Salumi

# Salumi

SAVORY RECIPES AND SERVING IDEAS FOR
SALAME, PROSCIUTTO, AND MORE

By John Piccetti and François Vecchio with Joyce Goldstein

*Foreword by David Rosengarten*

CHRONICLE BOOKS
SAN FRANCISCO

FOOD STYLIST: SANDRA COOK
PROP STYLIST: SARA SLAVIN
DESIGN BY FRANCES BACA

MANUFACTURED IN CHINA

CHRONICLE BOOKS LLC
680 SECOND STREET
SAN FRANCISCO, CALIFORNIA 94107

WWW.CHRONICLEBOOKS.COM

# Contents

# Primi . . . . . . . . . . . . . . . . . . . . . . . . . . . . 77
FIRST COURSES

# Secondi . . . . . . . . . . . . . . . . . . . . . . . . . . .101
MAIN COURSES

# Insalate e Contorni . . . . . . . . . . . . . . . 125
SALADS AND VEGETABLES

# Foreword

THE FASCINATING STORY OF SALUMI, as told by
the Columbus Salame Company of San Francisco, will be
of extreme interest to everyone around the world who
loves Italian food. In 1917, two Tuscan immigrants, Enrico
Parducci and Peter Domenici, arrived in North Beach,
the heart of the Italian community in San Francisco, and
founded a sausage company that grew, in less than one
hundred years, to grand proportions. What happened
along the way is the story of Italian food in America.

The founders called their pork products "sausage,"
a very general term for pork, fat, and seasonings stuffed
into casings. Later generations came to know it as
"salami," and across mid-twentieth-century America,
great lunch sandwiches and heroes were created with
it, while the Italian artisanal tradition, with all its
greater-than-"salami" variations and specifics, took a
back seat. For a time, "salami" ruled the land.

But then the modern Americans came along . . . the
passionate foodies, who just might want a "salami" hero
for lunch, but, who, that night, might want to serve their
dinner-party guests an array of artisanal salumi (very
specific, high-end variations on pork and fat in casings).

Doubly bless the Columbus Salame Company.
They have been here to provide what the people want—
whether hero fixings or high-level porcine creations.
And, now, they are here to explain it all in a gorgeous
book full of history and kitchen ideas—the only book

I know of with a full and accurate description of the
various, oft-confusing categories of artisanal salumi.

But there's so much more. In the history section,
you'll learn that Christopher Columbus (for whom the
company is named) actually brought the first salumi
to America! On the production side, you'll understand
that more coarsely chopped salumi has a fuller meat
flavor. In the discussion on style, you'll discover that
the "coatings" so popular on salumi today (black pepper,
herbs, etc.) are more French and American in nature
than they are Italian!

Best of all is the book's largest section, devoted to
great salumi cooking and serving ideas. Whether strictly
traditional or distinctly modern, the concepts presented
carry a relentlessly genuine Italian sensibility. With
a copy of this handsome book, complete with deeply
evocative photos, the time has passed when anyone
could possibly say, "What do I do with this stuff other
than slicing it and eating it?"

Of course, I hasten to point out that simply slicing
and eating salumi is one of the joys of my life, and I
remain forever in debt to the Columbus Salame Company
for the fabulously delicious opportunities they provide
to do so!

*David Rosengarten*
NEW YORK

# THE ART OF SALUMI

A TASTE OF THE PAST

THE HISTORY OF THE DIVINE PIG

THE HISTORY OF THE COLUMBUS SALAME COMPANY

SALUMI PRIMER

# A Taste of the Past

A MAN WALKED INTO an Italian delicatessen. He inhaled deeply and walked around the store slowly. The clerk asked, "May I help you?" The man replied, "I am just here to smell." The clerk replied, "No charge for that, sir."

The next time you walk into a delicatessen, instead of shopping with your eyes, first breathe deeply. Allow the symphony of aromas to lead you to the salumi counter. Next, look up at the various salami and prosciutti hanging from the ceiling. (In Italian, *salame* is singular and *salami* is plural, and these Italian spellings are used throughout the book.) Then let your eyes travel the length of the glass case, where dark red *coppa*, fat rounds of pistachio-studded mortadella, peppered pancetta, and plump sausages are arranged in tempting rows. Inhale the sweet, slightly funky aroma of cured meats, richly seasoned with garlic, cinnamon, nutmeg, cloves, black and red pepper, and other spices, along with the scent of pungent brined olives and of giant wheels of Parmigiano-Reggiano and *grana padano*—all of them products of long, careful aging.

The fragrant salumi of today's Italian delicatessen, or *salumeria*, grew out of the long-ago need to preserve meat. But necessity slowly evolved into an art form, and nowadays every Italian region has its own signature salumi, with small but significant variations that distinguish the products of one village from another, one

artisan from another, one family from another. In the past when Italians emigrated, they made great sacrifices. They gave up their homes, their language, and many of their social customs. But they seldom gave up their food.

Back home, the salumi makers, or *salumieri*, were primarily agrarian and depended on local farm animals and seasonal ingredients for what they made. In their new country, they couldn't depend on the same ingredients, so they had to modify their recipes. They kept whatever flavors they could from the past, dropped some ingredients and techniques, and added some new ones. The result was salumi that successfully married tradition, taste memory, and innovation.

In Italy, sausages, salami, and hams were—and many still are—salted and then air cured in the prevailing breezes. Modern refrigeration has eliminated the unpredictability that comes with relying on the weather, but the making of first-rate salumi depends on much more. Talent, skill, and experience are the key components— the indispensable "tools" that *salumieri* employ to seek out the finest meat and other ingredients and then combine them into a perfectly balanced mixture that will deepen in flavor with time. Each salame, each sausage is a little work of art and a symbol of the power of tradition and history. When we eat salumi, we eat a taste of the past.

# The History of the Divine Pig

ABOUT TEN THOUSAND YEARS ago, humans domesticated wild pigs, which proved remarkably easy. Pigs are intelligent, sociable animals that resist herding but like to be around people, making them good candidates for a lifestyle of settled farming. When bred in captivity, they are prolific, too. The average sow can produce two litters per year, with as many as a dozen piglets per litter. The newborns also gain weight at an amazing rate. A piglet that weighs 2 ½ pounds at birth can add 250 pounds in just six months.

Pigs have a highly developed sense of smell and hearing but poor eyesight. They lack sweat glands, so they like to live near shade and to cool down in water or mud. In the early days, pigs were foragers, roaming freely in densely shaded woodlands. Today in parts of Spain, Portugal, and Italy, the most desirable pigs still live on a diet of wild acorns that give the meat an aromatic sweetness.

Most scholars believe pigs were first domesticated in China and the Near East, and then spread to Europe, where they roamed freely all over Italy as early as 1000 BC. In the first century BC, the Roman scholar Varro penned instructions on how to feed and care for pigs to ensure they would yield the tastiest meat. Rome's pork markets were located near the city's salt markets,

and locals quickly learned how to salt and preserve the meat safely. The pig turned up regularly on the Roman banquet table, too, and in time the demand for pork outstripped supply, forcing Romans to import the difference from Gaul, modern-day France.

After the fall of Rome, the pig became the most important source of dietary meat in Europe. Each fall, farmers slaughtered their animals, cooked and ate a small portion of the meat fresh, and then preserved and stored the balance for eating the rest of the year. All over the continent, techniques unique to each region's palate were developed to salt, cure, and preserve pork.

Columbus introduced pigs to the New World on his second voyage in 1493, and they were soon being bred throughout the Caribbean and Latin America. In 1539, Spanish explorer Hernando de Soto brought thirteen sows and two boars to Florida, and within a year, the pig population had grown to three hundred. (Today, their offspring, known as razorbacks, freely roam the woods in Florida, West Virginia, Georgia, Arkansas, and the Carolinas.) Later expeditions to the Americas also included pigs in their cargo, introducing Italian, French, African, and British swine to the young country. As the American pioneers traveled west, their pigs went with them, and by the mid-1800s, pork was a significant

industry in Cincinnati (nicknamed Porkopolis) and
in Chicago, and the Midwest was well on its way to
becoming the center of the U.S. pork industry.

Today, the primary hog breeds in the United States
are Berkshire, Duroc, Chester White, Poland China,
Hampshire, Yorkshire, Spotted, and Landrace, with
most commercial production based on crossbreeding
for specific traits, such as a particularly meaty loin or a
large litter size. A pig weighing 250 pounds will yield
a carcass of about 185 pounds and average 100 pounds
of usable meat.

Nowadays, to satisfy the growing market for lean
meat, most mass-produced American pork has about
50 percent less fat than the pork of the 1950s, resulting
in ultralean meat ill-suited to making great salumi.
It is our belief that animals raised in a stress-free
environment, combined with favorable genetics and

Above: The signs of the Zodiac from a mosaic floor by Pantaleone
in the cathedral of Otranto, southern Italy. The mosaic shows
preparations for winter including chopping wood, storing food
and wine, and fattening a pig. The mosaic was completed in 1166.
PHOTOGRAPH BY ERICH LESSING, ART RESOURCE, NY

the allowance of the pigs to move freely according to
their natural behaviors, will produce higher-quality meat.

Responding to public demand, many smaller farmers are returning to the old-fashioned way of raising
pigs, humanely and sustainably, and are focusing on
heritage breeds known for their superior characteristics.
And skilled *salumieri*, who know that superior salumi
is possible only if the highest-quality pork is used, are
relying on the pork these farmers produce to make their
prized products. ◈

# The History of the Columbus Salame Company

AS TOLD BY JOHN PICCETTI  COLUMBUS

IN 1917, SAN FRANCISCO'S Italian neighborhood of North Beach welcomed a new member to its small community of immigrant business ventures. There, amid the sandlots and city streets where Joe DiMaggio would later hone his baseball wizardry, founding partners Enrico Parducci and Peter Domenici opened the San Francisco Sausage Company, choosing Columbus as their brand name, in tribute to the most widely recognized Italian in American history. They were confident

that the city's mild year-round climate, consistent humidity, and large Italian population offered the ideal conditions for a successful *salumificio*, or salame company.

Newly arrived immigrants from rural Tuscany, Parducci and Domenici came to America in the hope of providing a better life for their families. Living conditions in the Italian countryside were particularly difficult at the time, and the familiar climate and agricultural bounty of Northern California drew many Italians, especially from the north. Back home, Domenici had been an itinerant *salumiere*, or butcher and salame maker, traveling among villages and small towns. His trade was based on the Old World custom of small, family-owned shops hiring skilled *salumieri* to butcher whole pigs and make specialized products from the meat for the shops. Domenici brought this traditional art of producing salumi—prosciutti (cured hams), salami (cured sausages), and *salsiccie* (fresh sausages)—with him to San Francisco.

The first Columbus *salumificio* was at 505 Davis Street, in San Francisco's waterfront Produce District. Parducci

Above left: Exterior of the original San Francisco Sausage Company on Davis Street, circa 1925. Owners Enrico Parducci and Peter Domenici proudly pose with master and apprentice *salumieri*. An example of the opportunities the New World presented to these Italian Americans. PHOTOGRAPH COURTESY OF COLUMBUS FOODS LLC

and Domenici opened the doors and windows of their
shop to the temperate San Francisco air to create an ideal
curing environment for their salami. In the evening, fog
lightly bathed the curing rooms, the moist air playing its
own critical role in the drying and aging process.

In those early days, fresh pork was plentiful, provided
by small local farms. Well-fatted pigs were easily pro-
cured for the discerning sausage maker interested
in mature marbled meat, the key ingredient for high-
quality salumi. After careful trimming, lean pork
shoulder and firm pork fat were cut, mixed with spices,
and stuffed into natural casings of various shapes and
sizes. The type of casing used was (and still is) critical, as each lends a distinctive flavor and texture to the
salumi, in much the same way oak barrels from specific
forests add their unique character to the wine inside.

While Columbus Salame Company was standing
firm on Italian salumi traditions, it was also embracing
progress, looking for new ways to expand the young business. The first step was to seek a retail audience beyond
the Davis Street storefront. In the 1920s, Columbus
was selling its salami from its own storefront to delicatessens and grocery stores throughout the Bay Area.

As more customers learned about Columbus Salame,
the company earned a reputation for authenticity and
high quality that prompted the need for a larger production plant. In the 1930s, with Franklin D. Roosevelt
in the White House, Columbus moved to 447 Broadway
Street, in the heart of North Beach, where it continued
to manufacture its products through the Great Depres-
sion and World War II (you can still see the signage
painted on the wall near the roofline). Then, in 1946,
after almost thirty years, Parducci and Domenici retired
and sold Columbus Salame to the Devencenzi brothers,
John, Tony, Luis, and Victor.

Little more than a decade later, in 1957, the company
was purchased by six North Beach friends and family
members: Ernest DeMartini, Felix Gatto, Joseph Nave,
Albert Piccetti, John Poletti, and Roy Quilici. Under
the leadership of president Albert Piccetti, the small

Above: Interior of the original Davis Street *salumificio* with founding owners Parducci and Domenici in the foreground and future
owner Devencenzi in the background, circa 1930s. Note the fresh
pork carcasses being hand trimmed and boned by these experienced *salumieri*. PHOTOGRAPH COURTESY OF COLUMBUS FOODS LLC

local Broadway Street storefront business responded to
increasingly strict Federal regulations and continuing
demand for its products by building a state-of-the art
salame production facility in South San Francisco. The
owners weighed the considerable risks in moving into

## WHY THE NAME COLUMBUS?

WHILE THEIR BUSINESS competitors often
chose family surnames for their brands, founders
Enrico Parducci and Peter Domenici wanted their
company name to be symbolic of their pride
as Italian Americans. No name expressed their
intent better than the locally revered Christopher
Columbus. His name was already on Columbus
Avenue, which ran through the heart of San
Francisco's North Beach, home of Parducci and
Domenici's new company. Plus, the manifests of
the *Niña*, the *Pinta*, and the *Santa Maria* confirm
that Columbus brought the first salame to America.
Adopting Christopher Columbus as the company
name and icon was the only logical choice. Almost
a century later, his image and name still grace the
logo on Columbus Salame food products and are
emblazoned on every company delivery truck.

Above: The energetic young sons of the owners are pictured serving their apprenticeships on the manufacturing floor during their teenage years. From left to right, Gary DeMartini, Michael Gatto, John Piccetti, James Piccetti, and Philip Gatto. PHOTOGRAPH COURTESY OF COLUMBUS FOODS LLC

a new facility in an untried environment; and chose the new site for its felicitous microclimate of ocean and bay breezes that mimicked the temperature and humidity of North Beach.

In 1967, the city of San Francisco was experiencing the Summer of Love. The local nightclubs of Broadway Street were soon dominated by the topless craze of the era, and while our mothers were relieved to see Columbus relocate to South San Francisco, the new business park was a lot less interesting for their working teenage sons.

The company continued to grow and the second generation of the families gradually worked its way from the factory floor to managing the business, including Gary DeMartini, James Piccetti, myself, Michael Gatto, and future CEO Philip Gatto. In the 1980s, Columbus greatly expanded its regional footprint with the addition of multiple locations and a distribution facility.

The newest scientific and technological advances were pursued and incorporated into Columbus Salame's manufacturing processes. With modern Italian curing and aging technology as its model, Columbus pioneered specialty fermentation-starter cultures made available

through the work of Jim Bacus, PhD. During these years of dynamic growth, the Columbus reputation for quality was carried forward and maintained by a dedicated core of Italian immigrants led by Giovanni Oldini and Rolando Bertini, who together bring over a century of sausage-making skills and dedication to the workplace today.

My personal journey in the art of salumi began in the late 1980s through my working association with the Travaglini family of Milan, designers and manufacturers of curing technologies. It was during this period that I experienced the wonder of this most artful and ancient tradition of aging and curing specialty meats. My collaboration with a multi-talented Swiss *salumiere*, François Vecchio, quickly followed. This drive for Old World excellence was accelerated by an enthusiastic challenge from Philip Gatto. Together, François Vecchio, Gary DeMartini, and I created an exceptional level of artisan salumi without peer in the United States. This ultra-premium line necessitated searching out the best sources of raw materials and building a network of highest quality fresh meats and careful trimming by experienced meat cutters.

In addition to its traditional Italian salame products, Columbus has developed innovative "coated" salami that are more common to France and Germany than to Italy, including herb salame, pepper salame, hot fennel salame, and Cajun salame.

Today, several family members continue to push forward the dream of marketing authentic Old World salumi in America. Many of the owners have moved on to well deserved retirement, while new investments by parties that share the company's vision have been initiated to support more growth. I have assumed the role of Chairman of the Board, which gives me the opportunity to continue to impact these wonderful products I love so much. Based on Columbus' historic guiding principles of quality, I am proud to say, its future is bright. ◈

THE POET OF PORK

## THE POET OF PORK
# FRANÇOIS VECCHIO

FRANÇOIS VECCHIO HAS devoted more than fifty years of his life to making salumi, including training both *salumierie* and celebrity chefs in the art of curing meats. Born in Geneva, Switzerland, to a family of butchers and farmers, François was from the beginning surrounded by people who knew good food and whose livelihoods depended on it. His paternal grandfather was a cattle trader from Piedmont, his maternal grandfather a famous chef and restaurant owner in Geneva, and both of his grandmothers came from established farming families. His father was in the meat business, and at age twelve, François learned how to cut meat so he could participate in the annual hog harvest on the family farm. At eighteen, while attending business school, he began his formal three-year apprenticeship as a butcher. He continued his training in Germany and France, mastering wursts and charcuterie.

In 1960, François and two cousins were put in charge of the Vecchio Company, a well-established business in the Swiss meat trade, and they eventually acquired Rapelli, the largest *salumificio* in the Swiss canton of Ticino. Later, he became a consultant to GVS La Générale des Viandes et Salaisons, a venture led by a sugar company and the Rothschilds with the reorganization of the French meat industries its mandate. In 1972, François took one of the partners on a tour of the United States, visiting, by coincidence, Al Piccetti at Columbus Salame Company. Little did they know then that one day they would be working together.

In the early 1980s, François settled in the United States and founded a new salumi company, Rapelli of California. John Piccetti of Columbus, familiar with François's extensive experience and the quality of his work, invited him to be a consultant at Columbus, where he introduced new products that soon became staples in local delicatessens and markets.

In 2002, François also became a consultant for Niman Ranch, where Bill Niman and his partners were raising heritage pig breeds on over five hundred family-run farms the old-fashioned way, following protocols developed by the Animal Welfare Institute: without confinement, without antibiotics, and on a diet of soybean and field corn meal. The efforts by Niman Ranch set the standard for pork that was not "the other white meat" of the mass-market pork industry. It provided the well-fatted, rich meat used for the Columbus artisanal salumi line: *cacciatore, crespone, felino,* and *finocchiona.* This is now the fastest-growing segment of the Columbus business, reviving Old World traditions in a New World company.

# Salumi Primer

SALUMI IS THE GENERAL Italian term for cured meats, although some cooked meats are also included. The word comes from *sale*, or "salt," and a salumi selection includes *stagionati*, aged whole cuts such as hams (prosciutti) and pancetta, and *insaccati* (encased), cured seasoned chopped and ground meats in casings such as *salsicce* (sausages), mortadella, and salami. Almost all salumi are made from pork. Among the exceptions are *bresaola* (air-dried beef), popular in the Lombardian area of Valtellina, and some regional game and poultry specialties.

When it comes to the pig, or *maiale*, Italians are said to eat everything but the oink. The pork loin, chops, and ribs are roasted or braised. Select legs are used for making the famous Italian air-cured ham, or *prosciutto crudo*, while other legs are turned into cooked ham, or *prosciutto cotto*. The center cut of the ham is occasionally used for making *culatello*, a prized specialty of Emilia-Romagna. The pork belly becomes pancetta, rolled, cured, and aged bacon, and the pig's cheeks are transformed into *guanciale*. The fat is used for cooking or is cured and aged as *lardo*. It is no wonder the Italians refer to the pig as *il divin porcello*.

## Salumi Types

Here are brief descriptions of some classic Italian salumi—most of which the Columbus Salame Company produces according to authentic Italian traditions—and of a handful of Italian American salumi. They are all made from 100 percent pork. The items listed under the heading salame, all of them chopped meat stuffed into casings and then fermented and aged in special rooms, are known as *insaccati*, and generically referred to as salame. During aging, the salame develops a soft white coat of aromatic mold that protects it from excessive drying and enhances its flavor.

## Stagionati

PROSCIUTTO CRUDO is cured ham made from the hind leg of the pig. In Italy, a stamp on the rounded side of each ham attests to its being produced according to strict government regulations that control the genetics, raising, and processing of the hogs, as well as the final packaging for the consumer market. The best-known of these superior hams is *prosciutto di Parma*, from Emilia-Romagna. Other stellar examples include the darker and sweeter *prosciutto di San Daniele*, from a town in Friuli; and *prosciutto di Carpegna*, from an area in the Marches near Tuscany. In addition, many local artisans produce prosciutti according to their own regional traditions.

CULATELLO, a highly prized specialty of Emilia-Romagna, is made by salting a center cut taken from the finest ham and aging it for up to a year. The most famous is *culatello di Zibello*, produced in a small zone along the Po River. Most of the whole ham is sacrificed to make this smaller, pear-shaped, especially tender, and costly treat. *Culatello* is not exported from Italy.

**SPECK** is a smoked, boneless ham from Alto Adige, the alpine region of the South Tirol. It is typically seasoned with juniper berries, black pepper, and other spices.

**PANCETTA ARROTOLATA** is pork belly rolled, salt cured, seasoned with pepper and sweet spices, and hand tied for long, slow dry aging. Traditionally, it is a source of aromatic fat and meat for numerous dishes, from minestrone to pasta sauces. The equal proportions of fat and lean also make for an especially delicious filling for *panini* and a fine addition to salumi platters.

**GUANCIALE** is pig's cheek cured with salt and pepper. Its rich flavor is particularly appreciated by Roman cooks, who use it in two of their signature dishes, *spaghetti alla carbonara* and *bucatini all'amatriciana*. It is not exported, but some American chefs are now curing their own versions and offering them on their menus.

**LARDO**, pork fat salted and cured with herbs, is traditionally sliced paper-thin and served on warm bread to accentuate its creamy texture. Some of the most well-regarded producers are in Colonnata in Tuscany, Langhirano in Emilia-Romagna, and Arnad in the Valle d'Aosta, where it is cured with rosemary.

**COPPA** is a specialty of central and southern Italy, with distinctive versions produced from Umbria to Calabria to Puglia. Also known as *capocollo, coppa* is made from lean pork shoulder and is abundantly marbled with sweet fat. The meat is rubbed with salt, sugar, and spices, dry cured for two to three weeks, and then stuffed into casings and aged for up to a few months. The texture of *coppa* is more substantial than that of salame, and its flavor is stronger than that of prosciutto. Its dramatic appearance is particularly welcome on an antipasto platter. Mild black pepper and hot red pepper versions are available.

## Salame

**FELINO**, known as *il re di salumi italiani*, or "the king of Italian cured meats," comes from Emilia-Romagna, the same region that produces *prosciutto di Parma* and Parmigiano-Reggiano, and is made from the meat of pigs fed the whey left over from cheese making. A 1436 document drawn up in the city of Parma is the first written record of *felino*, but the salame probably dates to pre-Roman times. Its particularly thick pork casing allows for exceptionally long aging, which yields a product with a complex aroma and flavor—akin to what wine makers call a long finish. Top producers use the best-quality hand-trimmed pork shoulder, which is coarsely chopped and mixed with sweet white wine, garlic, and black pepper. Each *felino* is tied by hand and weighs between 1 ½ and 2 ½ pounds.

**CRESPONE** is a country-style salame from the Lombardian area of Brianza, which lies between Milan and the Alps in northern Italy and is home to some of Italy's finest *salumieri*. It is made from hand-trimmed, coarsely chopped pork shoulder seasoned with sweet white wine, garlic, and black pepper, stuffed into a casing, and tied by hand. Slow aging and mild fermentation give *crespone*, which usually weighs between ¾ and 1 ½ pounds, a particularly rich flavor.

**FINOCCHIONA TOSCANA** is a particularly tender salame that is sometimes called *sbriciolona* (from *sbriciolare*, "to crumble") because it is delicate and crumbles easily when cut. (Don't confuse it with *finocchiata*, a cured pork loin sausage with pepper and wild fennel.) *Finocchiona* takes its name from *finocchio*, or "fennel," which is what gives the salame its distinctive sweet flavor and aroma. At Columbus, coarsely chopped pork is flavored with wine, whole wild fennel seeds, garlic, and black pepper and then stuffed into a special double-layered natural pork casing that is hand stitched together to achieve the final hefty size. With a finished weight of seven to ten pounds, this salame requires a minimum of three months of careful aging to acquire its perfect bouquet. It can be cut paper-thin—the large slices are spectacular on an antipasto platter—or into small cubes, and is a good addition to salads.

**CACCIATORE** and **SECCHI** are also known as *salametti* because of their small size. Just one inch in diameter and with a thin casing, they call for brief fermentation and aging of only about three weeks. They weigh four to six ounces each and are hand tied in long chains of twelve. *Cacciatore*, which means "hunter," is named for its portability in a pocket or backpack. It is made from coarsely chopped pork, wine, garlic, and pepper and is stuffed into a delicate natural casing. Due to their light fermentation, *cacciatori* are extremely mild and aromatic. To fully appreciate their texture and taste, cut them into slices $1/8$ inch thick, with or without the edible casing in place. The name *secchi*, which means "dry," was coined by Italian Americans in San Francisco for a locally created artisanal product similar to the *salametti* of Italy. *Secchi* marries finely ground pork, salt, wine, garlic, black pepper, nutmeg, and touch of sugar to produce a mild, well-balanced flavor and a smooth mouthfeel. Enjoy it with or without its traditional thin, natural casing.

**SALAME TOSCANO**, which is about four inches in diameter, is made from lean pork finely chopped to a paste and mixed with black pepper, mace, and *lardelli*, small strips of pork fat. When the salame is sliced, the white fat offers a striking visual contrast to the rich, red lean meat.

**SOPRESSATA** (also spelled *soprassata* and *soppressata*) has many regional variations. In the Veneto, it is made with coarsely cut pork shoulder meat and fat and spiced with pepper, garlic, and red wine. In the rustic Abruzzese version, the coarsely cut pork is seasoned with red wine, fennel seeds, red pepper flakes, garlic, and black pepper. In Calabria, where it is soft and spicy from a mixture of black pepper and the local hot red *peperoncino*,

*sopressata* is stuffed into large casings that are pressed into oblong shapes over the course of a medium fermentation and relatively long aging. This combination of spices and acidity yields a highly complex aroma and a pleasantly spicy finish. It is typically served cut into slices or into cubes.

## Italian American Salame

**MILANO SALAME** was adapted in San Francisco's North Beach by Italian immigrants, and nowadays in America is regarded as the classic "Italian dry" salame. The pork is finely chopped, richly flavored with wine, garlic, black pepper, mace, and nutmeg, and then strongly fermented to give the salame a nice bite. Milano salame is firm and is usually sliced thin, deli style, making it a great sandwich meat.

**GENOA SALAME**, named for the birthplace of Christopher Columbus, combines finely chopped pork, salt, sugar, red wine, a bit of garlic, black pepper, and a touch of mace. The mixture is stuffed into a large-diameter casing and then fermented and aged for up to two months to yield an especially soft texture and mild flavor. It is best served thinly sliced.

**CALABRESE HOT SALAME** is based on a traditional recipe from Calabria, where spicy cured and fresh sausages are widely enjoyed. The addition of *peperoncini* and paprika to finely ground pork give the salame its characteristic ruby red color and sweet pepper flavor.

## Cooked Salumi

**MORTADELLA** originated in Bologna, in Emilia-Romagna, and is in great demand on the Italian table. It is made by adding tasty cubes of blanched tender pork fat to an emulsion of lean pork shoulder spiced with coriander, nutmeg, and cracked black pepper, and is available with or without the traditional whole pistachios. This large salumi demands long cooking in a dry-air oven, preceded by a brief curing and fermenting phase. It is usually enjoyed very thinly sliced or cut into cubes, and is also excellent lightly grilled like a steak and served hot.

**SALAME COTTO** is a traditional alternative to classic dry salame. *Cotto* means "cooked," and *salame cotto* is pork seasoned with cracked black pepper, wine, nutmeg, and cinnamon, and then fully cooked.

**PROSCIUTTO COTTO**, or "cooked ham," is made by boning and trimming a leg to yield the whole muscles, briefly curing the pork in a salt brine, molding it, and then slowly cooking it. The result is a tender, pink ham with a delicious layer of external fat.

**COTECHINO** is a fresh pork sausage made from the lean meat of the head and neck and is always served cooked. A specialty of Modena and Cremona, it is long simmered and then typically served with lentils, boiled beans, or mashed potatoes. Modena's other traditional sausage, *zampone*, made from essentially the same ingredients but stuffed into a boned pig's trotter, is also long cooked and served hot.

# Curing Salumi

Curing salumi requires skill and time. The process must begin with well muscled and fatted meat from healthy animals. After the meat is trimmed, salted, spiced, and put into casings, maintaining the proper temperature and humidity is crucial to promoting the correct fermentation and subsequent aging and maturation.

Properly cured meat goes through two stages. The critical first stage, which includes curing and fermenting, lasts about one week. During this time, natural moisture is drawn out of the meat, which sets the reddish color and concentrates the flavors. In the second, or aging, stage, the meat's natural enzymes, aided by beneficial bacterial cultures, break down low-flavor protein and fats into high-flavor amino acids. The moisture continues to reduce and the characteristic—and vital—penicillium mold begins to grow on the exterior of the casing. This mold, called *fiore*, or "bloom," in Italian, acts as a natural antioxidant and protects against rancidity. As long as the mold is present, the rich flavors of the meat will continue to develop. This is why the mold on the most authentic salame is always kept intact until serving, and why it would be rare to find an Italian eating a product without mold.

Every traditionally cured salame generates a mold on the outside of its casing during fermentation and aging. While modern processors employ science to maintain an aesthetically pleasing white mold, nature on its own will normally generate an artist's palette of colors. The mold adds to the overall aroma and complexity of a salame, playing a role similar to that of the dusty white coating on such popular mold-ripened cheeses as Brie and Camembert. Salumi makers encourage those benefits by aging their freshly made salami in special curing rooms kept at a precise temperature and humidity level. When a salame is market-ready, the excess mold is airbrushed away.

It takes roughly three weeks for the smallest salame to cure and dry fully. A midsized salame will be ready in five to six weeks, and the largest-diameter salame will take up to three months. During the dry aging process, each salame, regardless of size, will lose a minimum of one-third of its original weight.

The curing process is the result of a team of naturally occurring living organisms that are responsible for creating fermentation in a host of familiar foods, including salami, cheeses, yogurt, bread, beer, and wine. In the past, people relied solely on these naturally occurring beneficial bacteria, but today manufacturers have refined this process by using starter cultures grown under controlled conditions that guarantee product consistency and safety.

Salt is the most essential ingredient for curing meat. It speeds up the dehydration process and reduces the amount of water that would otherwise allow bacteria to grow and spoil the meat. Salt also enhances flavor. Today's commercial curing mixtures are refined to include sodium nitrite and sodium nitrate, which acts like a time-release form of sodium nitrite and is essential for long curing. The nitrates turn into nitrites and eventually dissipate as nitrous oxide over time, yielding sweet-tasting salami with rich color and complex flavors. The growth of lactic acid bacteria increases the acidity of the meat mixture, which inhibits the growth of harmful bacteria. A manufacturer must ferment any salame to a pH below 5.3 within a given number of hours that changes with the temperature. (The higher the temperature, the faster the salame must be fermented to achieve the target pH.)

## Salumi in Moderation

Many of us are watching our fat intake these days, so concern about the fat content of salumi is natural. The answer, of course, is to enjoy it in moderation. Salumi is so rich and flavorful that a little goes a long way toward providing satisfaction. Also, the percentage of fat in a salame is exaggerated when compared to the fat in other foods because aging causes concentration. Meats sold raw declare their percentage of fat before cooking or drying, and therefore use the moisture content to depress the percentage of overall fat. In contrast, a salame loses one-third of its weight through fermentation and aging, which produces a higher fat percentage.

To understand this, you must keep in mind that the fat to protein ratio is the relevant nutritional value. For example, a typical cut of fresh pork contains 22 percent fat and 78 percent lean meat. As a salame ages, these naturally occurring proportions are altered because of moisture loss that occurs only in the lean

portion. When the aging process is complete, the salame will have been reduced to 67 percent of its original weight. But the proportions of both fat and protein will have increased relative to weight because the fat to protein ratio remains the same despite moisture loss. Much the same thing happens when aging such cheeses as Parmigiano-Reggiano and *grana padano* or when drying nuts and seeds.

While olive oil and other healthier fats exist, pork fat is not as harmful as some consumers believe. It has about 50 percent less saturated fat than palm oil and about 40 percent less than butter. It also has twice the monounsaturated fat of butter. Following a healthy Mediterranean diet, Italians eat salumi in small portions, accompanied by bread, fruit, vegetables, and grains to balance the rich, concentrated flavors of the meat. This is an exemplary model for dining.

## Quality is in the Details

Many consumers believe that all Italian salami are pretty much the same, but this is far from accurate. Commercial "hard" salami are often combinations of pork and beef, produced under a least cost basis, which alters the meat formulations continuously to take advantage of lower market costs. The inherent quality of specific cuts and their unique characteristics are normally lost in this cost driven mindset of sausage production. Typically, they are heavily spiced and fermented at higher temperatures to speed aging, which precludes the development of mold and the complexity that is achieved by lower temperature and longer time processes. Salame produced in this fashion just cannot achieve the complexity, aroma, and clean finish in the palate as traditionally produced product.

In contrast, to make traditional Italian-style salami, the *salumiere* must purchase high-quality meat from prime hogs and select the choicest cuts of lean and hard fat. Skilled workers must be hired to cut and trim the pork to stringent specifications. Salami of artisanal quality also require the best natural casings. Although more expensive, they allow for better fermentation and longer aging. For example, the typical cellulose casing used for most precut products costs about $0.10 per pound of salame, while a natural casing is about $1.12 per pound. Add in the costs of good wine and fresh spices, and the absence of fillers and additives, and you can understand why these salami cost more.

Assembling the finest ingredients is just part of the story, however. Just as in the Old Country, trained *salumieri* in the United States know how to use their eyes, nose, hands, and taste buds to judge when a salame is at its peak of flavor. They know the proper feel of the meat as it ages, and the texture, firmness, and aroma that signify when the salame is "ripe," and thus ready for the consumer. Less-experienced workers might miss that window, either by misjudging the sense indicators or rushing through the process, but true craftsmen invariably get it right.

Yet the most expensive ingredient in the making of quality salumi is time. These prized meats demand slower fermentation and longer aging than their industrially produced counterparts, much as fine wines require additional cellaring to reach their peak. Both the cost of the physical space and of the labor needed to monitor the maturation adds to the overall cost of the product. And just as restaurants charge more for the reserve wines that stay in their cellars until they reach maximum flavor, the producers of quality salumi must reflect the cost of curing and aging in the price of their products.

# Buying, Storing, and Serving

## How to Buy Salami

Now that you understand how these artisanal products are made, you need to know what to look for when buying them. Here are the five standards by which every product should be evaluated: ingredients, appearance, aroma, texture, and taste.

Just as in fine cooking, the fewer unnecessary ingredients, the better the product. So, start by reading the ingredients list on the label. The main ingredient should be pork. If both pork and beef are listed, this is a sign of a nontraditional, lesser-quality product. Check for added water, artificial color, soy protein, starches, preservatives, and other extenders, all undesirable ingredients in the best-quality salame. A very small amount of nonfat milk powder is an acceptable addition in some products.

Next, look at the appearance. In the case of whole salami, the surface should have a light coating of grayish white mold. They should look plump, filling out their casing, and should "give" a bit when squeezed. Overdried, poorly stored salami will have lost their essential moisture. In the case of sliced, packaged salame, look for a rich, reddish color that is even and consistent. Any quality presliced product should exhibit the same excellence as a product you have sliced for you at a full-service delicatessen.

Bring the salame to your nose and inhale. The aroma of a well-made salame is sweet, spicy, meaty, and appealing. Cut a slice and look at the knife. There should be no trail of fat on the blade. Then take a bite of the slice and consider texture and mouthfeel. Just as a fine extra virgin olive oil will never feel oily in your mouth, a quality salame should never taste greasy. Instead, as the Italians say, *Il buon salame lascia la bocca pulita* (A good salame leaves the mouth clean).

Now, consider the flavor. It should be round, complex, earthy, full of character, and balanced. The first thing you should taste is the sweet pork. Garlic and spices should be perceptible but not dominant. Salame that is more coarsely chopped will have a fuller meat flavor because of its longer curing time. Like fine wine, the salame should have a long finish, with its flavors lingering on your palate.

## How to Store Salumi

Uncut molded salami, such as *sopressata* and *felino*, are best kept in a cool, dry area, ideally conditions similar to those of a wine cellar. Since most of us do not have a cellar, the refrigerator is the next best choice. Wrap whole salami in butcher paper, freezer paper, or, as a last resort, waxed paper, and store in the meat drawer or on the coldest shelf. Avoid plastic wrap, because it can trap moisture on the casing (note: companies are researching a perforated, breathable plastic wrap that would work as well as butcher paper). Molded products continue to age, causing changes in their taste, texture, and dryness, so how long you keep them depends on personal taste. Keep in mind that because *salametti* are small, their shelf life will be shorter than for large salami. Once a salame is cut, rewrap it in butcher or other paper and return it to the refrigerator. Be sure always to "face" the product (throw away the first slice, which has been exposed to air) before cutting more to serve. A cut salame should usually be consumed within thirty to sixty days.

Keep vacuum-packed packages of presliced salame refrigerated and consume the contents by the sell-by date on the package. Once opened, rewrap carefully in plastic wrap and consume within five to seven days. If you have purchased sliced salame, prosciutto, or pancetta at your local delicatessen, overwrap the package with plastic wrap and store in the coldest part of the refrigerator. Prosciutto keeps well for up to three days, while salame, mortadella, and pancetta will keep well for five to seven days.

## How to Peel and Slice Salame

While eating the exterior mold is not harmful, the salame casing is generally peeled away from the meat before serving. Exceptions are *cacciatore* and *secchi*, which have thin, delicate natural casings that are usually eaten along with the meat. Presliced packaged salame is sold with the casing already removed, so the slices are ready to eat.

If the salame has a fibrous or collagen casing (the salame will have a uniform, cylindrical shape), it should peel with ease. Using a sharp knife, cut the end of the salame and peel away just enough casing to expose the amount of salame you need, keeping the remainder of the casing intact.

If the salame has a natural casing (the salame will have an irregular, curvy shape), wrap it in a damp paper towel for five minutes. This will rehydrate the casing and encourage it to pull away from the meat. Then, using a sharp knife, cut the end of the salame and peel away the casing, again exposing only the amount of salame you plan to serve.

To slice a salame, use your sharpest, thin-bladed knife, though never one with a serrated blade (it can tear the meat), or use a meat slicer. If you are cutting by hand, keeping the slices uniform is difficult, especially when cutting small or irregularly shaped products, so an electric slicer is best. The thickness of the cut affects the taste of the salame, and personal preferences vary. Some aficionados say thin slices are best in all cases. Others insist smaller-diameter products, such as *cacciatore*, should be cut about $1/8$ inch thick, and larger-diameter products, such as *sopressata*, should be about $1/16$ inch thick. The latter recommendation follows what is known as the Italian rule: Slice large products thinly, so the slices are thin enough to roll up easily, and slice smaller ones slightly thicker, or just substantial enough to give pleasing resistance when you bite. With quality salami, you want to taste the meat, so if you slice them a bit thicker, you just need to chew them more slowly—and you'll enjoy them a bit longer.

## How to Serve Salumi

Many Americans are used to making sandwiches by piling chilled cheese, salame, and other cured meats on bread with mustard, mayonnaise, pickles, cold lettuce, and cold tomatoes. But chilling foods mutes their distinctive tastes. To appreciate the complex flavors and aromas of salumi, you must serve them at room temperature.

In Italy, cheeses and salumi are served in small portions of one to two ounces per person, often with olives and a simple antipasto salad or two alongside. *Grissini* (bread sticks) or rustic bread is typically offered as an accompaniment, sometimes with sweet butter, its creaminess playing beautifully off the cured meats. Or, the salumi is matched with fruit, in a pleasing contrast of salt and sweet. If you enjoy the classic food pairing of prosciutto and melon or prosciutto and figs, salame,

with its more pronounced spice notes, is wonderful with thin slivers of pear or with figs or grapes.

The Italians respect the artisanal character of salumi, and thus consume it in moderation and with appreciation for the time and craftsmanship that has gone into making it. We see the value in the Italian model and recommend that you approach your consumption of it the same way. For quick and easy serving ideas, see the Shop and Serve Antipasti features sprinkled throughout this book. You can also use salumi in your cooking, as you will discover in the recipe chapters that follow.

# RECIPES

# Antipasti e Spuntini

## ANTIPASTI AND SNACKS

THE FORMAL ITALIAN MEAL opens with one or more antipasti. In the past, in prosperous homes and especially in restaurants, the course was often an elaborate assortment of small plates. But nowadays, just one or two simple plates typically launch a meal at home, or sometimes a bountiful array of antipasti becomes the meal itself.

The antipasto course can be as uncomplicated as a platter of assorted salumi, a cheese or two, some olives, and a basket of rustic bread. You might add a condiment to the table as well, such as Caponata (page 44), an onion *conserva* (page 47), or *peperonata* (page 42). Or, you can pair prosciutto and/or other salumi with slices of ripe pear or melon, fresh figs, a bunch of grapes, or a crock of warm herb-laced ricotta (page 38). Pour a chilled Prosecco, Lambrusco or another sparkling wine, or a crisp Pinot Grigio or Tocai Friulano—all complementary partners for rich salumi and their accompaniments.

A bruschetta, a slice of frittata, a rice croquette, or a slim wedge cut from a rich meat-and-cheese pie also makes a fine antipasto. Any one of them makes a satisfying snack, too, as does a pizza or a *panino*, all of which are in this chapter. Beyond these pages, you will find several Shop and Serve Antipasti ideas, easy-to-assemble antipasti that star a variety of salumi and call for no—or minimal—cooking, making them the ideal choice for the busy host.◉

# Ricotta infornata alle erbe

**BAKED RICOTTA WITH HERBS**

A crock of baked ricotta, warm and creamy, pairs well with a platter of salumi. For the best results, seek out a soft, mildly sweet fresh ricotta from a local cheese artisan. Accompany the warm cheese with grilled or toasted bread for spreading.   **WINE** Pinot Grigio or Sauvignon Blanc   **SERVES** 6

2 CUPS (ABOUT 1 POUND) FRESH WHOLE-MILK
   RICOTTA CHEESE
3 TABLESPOONS CHOPPED FRESH SAGE OR ROSEMARY
SALT AND FRESHLY GROUND BLACK PEPPER
EXTRA VIRGIN OLIVE OIL FOR DRIZZLING
TOASTED OR GRILLED COARSE COUNTRY BREAD
   FOR SERVING

Preheat the oven to 300°F. Lightly oil a 3-cup ovenproof crock. In a bowl, stir the cheese well with a fork until smooth. Mix in the sage and season to taste with salt and pepper. Pack the cheese into the prepared crock, and drizzle a little olive oil on top.

Bake until heated through and the center quivers a bit when the crock is lightly shaken, about 15 minutes. Serve warm with toasted bread.

# Ricotta al forno

BAKED RICOTTA

Here is another version of baked ricotta that is an equally good partner for a platter of salumi. This one sets up as it bakes, and then is unmolded and sliced. Have a crusty loaf of hearth-baked bread on hand to accompany both the cheese and the cured meats. **WINE** Pinot Grigio or Sauvignon Blanc **SERVES** 8 to 10

4 CUPS (ABOUT 2 POUNDS) FRESH WHOLE-MILK
    RICOTTA CHEESE

2 TABLESPOONS UNSALTED BUTTER, AT ROOM
    TEMPERATURE

¼ CUP FINE DRIED BREAD CRUMBS

4 EGGS

½ CUP GRATED PARMESAN CHEESE

⅔ CUP PITTED OIL-CURED BLACK OLIVES,
    COARSELY CHOPPED

½ TEASPOON SALT

1 TEASPOON FRESHLY GROUND BLACK PEPPER

EXTRA VIRGIN OLIVE OIL FOR DRIZZLING

If the ricotta cheese contains a lot of moisture, spoon it into a sieve placed over a bowl and let drain for about 1 hour at room temperature.

Preheat the oven 375°F. Rub a 2-quart soufflé dish or charlotte mold or an 8-inch springform pan with the butter, and then sprinkle with the bread crumbs, tapping out the excess crumbs.

In a bowl, combine the ricotta, eggs, and Parmesan and mix well. Stir in the olives, salt, and pepper. (You don't need much salt because both the Parmesan and olives are salty.) Transfer the mixture to the prepared dish.

Bake until golden on top and firm to the touch, 1 to 1 ¼ hours. Let cool for a few minutes, then invert a plate on top, invert the dish and plate together, and lift off the dish. The mold will sink a bit. Cut into wedges, drizzle with olive oil, and serve warm.

# Funghi marinati

## MARINATED MUSHROOMS

These mushrooms brighten any antipasto assortment, but especially one that includes a selection of salumi. Be careful not to marinate the mushrooms too long, as you want them to have some crunch. If you don't finish them, they can be covered and refrigerated for a few days and then brought to room temperature before serving, though they will be softer. **WINE** Prosecco or Lambrusco **SERVES** 8

½ CUP EXTRA VIRGIN OLIVE OIL

⅔ CUP RED WINE VINEGAR

2 CLOVES GARLIC, CRUSHED

1 TABLESPOON SUGAR

1 TEASPOON SALT

¼ CUP WATER

1 SMALL YELLOW ONION, CUT INTO ¼-INCH-THICK
   SLICES AND SEPARATED INTO RINGS

⅔ POUND FRESH SMALL WHITE BUTTON OR CREMINI
   MUSHROOMS

In a deep bowl, whisk together the olive oil, vinegar, garlic, sugar, salt, and water until the sugar and salt dissolve. Add the onion rings, turn to coat, and set aside.

Using a paring knife, trim away the stem ends on the mushrooms, and then wipe the mushrooms clean with damp paper towels. Add the mushrooms to the marinade, stir gently to mix well, and leave uncovered at room temperature for about 4 hours before serving.

Serve the mushrooms with toothpicks for spearing.

# Involtini di melanzane

## STUFFED EGGPLANT ROLLS

Eggplant is versatile and turns up often on the antipasto table. These little rolls, filled with prosciutto and cheese, are a particularly flavorful way to serve it. Do not cut the eggplant slices too thin for these rolls, as the eggplant will shrink during cooking. Grilling the slices will add a pleasant smokiness that marries well with the prosciutto and mozzarella filling. But if you don't want to light the grill, you can fry the slices in olive oil with equally good results.  **WINE** Aglianico or Fiano d'Avellino  **SERVES** 8 to 10

2 GLOBE EGGPLANTS, PEELED AND SLICED LENGTHWISE
⅓ INCH THICK (18 TO 20 SLICES)

½ CUP EXTRA VIRGIN OLIVE OIL (FOR FRYING), PLUS
AS NEEDED

SALT AND FRESHLY GROUND BLACK PEPPER

10 LONG, THIN SLICES PROSCIUTTO, CUT IN HALF
CROSSWISE AND EACH HALF TRIMMED TO FIT THE
EGGPLANT SLICES AFTER COOKING

20 STRIPS FRESH MOZZARELLA CHEESE, ½ INCH WIDE
AND THICK AND 1 ½ TO 2 INCHES LONG

20 FRESH MINT LEAVES, CUT INTO NARROW STRIPS

SALT AND FRESHLY GROUND BLACK PEPPER

To grill the eggplant slices, prepare a hot fire in a grill. When the fire is ready, brush the eggplant slices on both sides with the olive oil and sprinkle with salt and pepper. Place the eggplant slices directly over the fire and grill, turning once, until tender but not too soft, about 4 minutes total. Remove from the grill.

To fry the eggplant slices, layer them in a colander, lightly salting each layer, and let stand for 30 minutes to release excess water. Pat the eggplant slices completely dry with paper towels. In a sauté pan, warm ½ cup olive oil over medium heat. Working in batches, add the eggplant slices and fry, turning once, until translucent and tender but not too soft, 6 to 8 minutes total. Transfer to paper towels to drain.

Preheat the oven to a 400°F. Lightly oil a baking dish large enough to accommodate the rolls in a single layer without crowding.

To assemble each roll, top an eggplant slice with a prosciutto slice, a strip of mozzarella, and a scattering of mint. Roll up the slice and secure with a toothpick if it threatens to unroll. Arrange the rolls, seam side down, in the prepared dish. Drizzle lightly with olive oil.

Bake the rolls just long enough to melt the cheese, about 15 minutes. Arrange the rolls on a platter and remove the toothpicks, if used. Serve warm, while the cheese is still soft.

# Mandorlata di peperoni

## SWEET-AND-SOUR PEPPERS WITH ALMONDS

This colorful dish of sautéed peppers, also known as *peperonata*, comes from the southern Italian regions of Calabria and Basilicata, home of robust *sopressata*, hot *coppa*, and spicy fresh sausages. It is usually served at room temperature as part of a large antipasto assortment, but you need nothing more than the bold flavors of an array of salumi to show off its sweet, mildly tart notes.   **WINE** Barbera, Dolcetto d'Alba, or Lambrusco   **SERVES** 8

2 LARGE YELLOW BELL PEPPERS

2 LARGE RED BELL PEPPERS

6 TABLESPOONS OLIVE OIL

1 LARGE OR 2 SMALL RED ONIONS, CUT INTO ¼-INCH-THICK SLICES

3 CLOVES GARLIC, MINCED

¼ CUP RED WINE VINEGAR, OR AS NEEDED

1 TABLESPOON SUGAR, OR AS NEEDED

6 TABLESPOONS THICK TOMATO PUREE

¼ CUP RAISINS, PLUMPED IN HOT WATER AND DRAINED

¼ CUP SLIVERED BLANCHED ALMONDS, TOASTED

SALT

Cut the yellow and red peppers in half lengthwise and remove the stems, seeds, and thick membranes. Cut the halves lengthwise into strips about ⅓ inch wide.

In a large sauté pan, warm the olive oil over medium heat. Add the onion and garlic and cook, stirring occasionally, until the onion is beginning to soften, about 5 minutes. Toss in the peppers and cook, stirring occasionally, until the peppers are nearly tender, about 8 minutes. Add the vinegar, sugar, and tomato puree and cook for about 3 minutes longer to blend the flavors.

Add the raisins and almonds, stir well, and season lightly with salt. Taste and adjust the seasoning with more salt, sugar, and/or vinegar. This dish should have a nice balance of tartness and sweetness, and the vegetables should be tender but not mushy. Remove from the heat and serve warm or at room temperature. The *peperonata* will keep, tightly covered, in the refrigerator for up to 4 days; bring to room temperature before serving.

# Caponata

## SWEET-AND-SOUR EGGPLANT

If possible, make this signature dish of Sicily a day or two ahead of time to allow the flavors to marry. Before serving, bring to room temperature and taste and adjust the seasoning, adding more vinegar, sugar, and/or salt. Serve in a bowl alongside a platter of salumi.  **WINE** Tocai Friulano, Sauvignon Blanc, or Nero d'Avola  **SERVES** 8

2 LARGE GLOBE EGGPLANTS, PEELED AND CUT INTO
  ³/₄-INCH CUBES

SALT

ABOUT 1 ½ CUPS EXTRA VIRGIN OLIVE OIL

1 CUP DICED CELERY

2 YELLOW ONIONS, CUT INTO ¼-INCH-THICK SLICES

1 CUP TOMATO PUREE

3 TABLESPOONS CAPERS, PREFERABLY SALT
  PACKED, RINSED

15 TO 20 PITTED GREEN OLIVES, COARSELY CHOPPED

¼ CUP PINE NUTS, SLIVERED BLANCHED ALMONDS, OR
  PISTACHIOS, TOASTED

½ CUP RED WINE VINEGAR

2 TABLESPOONS SUGAR, OR AS NEEDED

FRESHLY GROUND BLACK PEPPER

3 TABLESPOONS CHOPPED FRESH BASIL OR FLAT-LEAF
  PARSLEY (OPTIONAL)

Layer the eggplant cubes in a colander, lightly salting each layer. Let stand for 30 minutes to release excess water. Pat the cubes completely dry with paper towels and set aside.

In a large, wide, deep sauté pan, warm a few tablespoons of the olive oil over medium heat. Add the celery and sauté just until beginning to soften, 2 to 3 minutes. It should still be crisp. Using a slotted spoon, transfer to a bowl and set aside.

Return the sauté pan to medium-high heat and add ½ cup of the olive oil. When the oil is hot, add half of the eggplant cubes and cook, turning often, until translucent, 6 to 8 minutes. Using the slotted spoon, transfer the eggplant to a second bowl and set aside. Repeat with the remaining eggplant, adding more oil (¼ to ½ cup) as needed to prevent scorching.

Reduce the heat under the sauté pan to medium. If the pan is dry, add a few tablespoons olive oil. Add the onions and cook, stirring occasionally, until softened and translucent but not browned, about 10 minutes. Return the celery to the pan, add the tomato puree, and simmer for 10 minutes to blend and concentrate the flavors. Return the cooked eggplant to the pan and add the capers, olives, nuts, vinegar, and sugar and simmer for 20 minutes to blend the flavors.

Season to taste with salt and pepper and with more sugar, if needed. Remove from the heat, stir in the basil, transfer to a bowl, and let cool. Serve at room temperature. The eggplant will keep, tightly covered, in the refrigerator for up to 5 days; bring to room temperature before serving.

# Cipolline in agrodolce

## SWEET-AND-SOUR ONIONS

The cooks of the Veneto regularly prepare onions in *agrodolce*, or sweet-and-sour sauce, for serving as an antipasto or a *contorno* (vegetable side dish), adding raisins and pine nuts that intensify the natural sweetness of the onions. You can use any type of small onion in any color—white, yellow, or red. *Cipolline*, small, flat, oval onions native to Italy, are a good choice here.  **WINE** Valpolicella or Merlot     **SERVES** 8

2 POUNDS SMALL WHITE, YELLOW, OR RED ONIONS
   SUCH AS PEARL OR BOILING, 1 TO 1 ½ INCHES IN
   DIAMETER, OR SLIGHTLY LARGER *CIPOLLINE*

6 TABLESPOONS OLIVE OIL

2 TABLESPOONS SUGAR

6 TABLESPOONS RED WINE VINEGAR OR
   3 TABLESPOONS EACH RED WINE VINEGAR
   AND BALSAMIC VINEGAR

1 TABLESPOON TOMATO PASTE (OPTIONAL)

¼ CUP RAISINS

¼ CUP PINE NUTS, TOASTED

SALT

Trim the root end of each onion carefully, leaving the bottom of the bulb intact, then cut a shallow cross in the root end to prevent the onion from telescoping during cooking. Bring a large saucepan filled with water to a boil. Add the onions and boil until barely cooked, about 5 minutes, then drain. The onions should still be firm. When cool enough to handle, slip off and discard the skins.

In a large sauté pan, warm the olive oil over medium heat. Add the onions and cook, stirring occasionally, until golden brown on all sides, about 8 minutes. Reduce the heat to low and add the sugar, vinegar, tomato paste, and raisins. Cover the pan tightly and simmer until the onions are fork-tender, 25 to 30 minutes, depending on their size. Uncover and stir in the pine nuts.

Season to taste with salt and transfer the onions to a serving dish. Serve warm or at room temperature. Offer toothpicks for spearing the onions. The onions will keep, tightly covered, in the refrigerator for up to 4 days; bring to room temperature before serving.

# Marmellata di cipolle rosse

### RED ONION MARMALADE

In southern Italy, the sweet red Tropea onion of Calabria is typically used for making this full-flavored marmalade, which is delicious spread on bread, topped with slices of salumi, and served with a glass of Lambrusco or Valpolicella. The onion itself has long been prized for its medicinal properties—a cure for colds and flus, a tonic for bad circulation, and a remedy for dozens of other maladies—making this *conserva* both healthful and delicious. **MAKES** 3 to 4 cups

ABOUT ½ CUP OLIVE OIL

6 LARGE RED ONIONS, THINLY SLICED

1 CUP SUGAR

2 CUPS RED WINE VINEGAR

1 TEASPOON MUSTARD SEEDS (OPTIONAL)

1 TABLESPOON GRATED ORANGE ZEST (OPTIONAL)

FRESHLY GROUND BLACK PEPPER

In a large sauté pan, warm the olive oil over low heat. Add the onions and cook, stirring often, until softened, about 20 minutes. Add the sugar, vinegar, mustard seeds, and orange zest and simmer until almost all of the liquid has evaporated and the onions are syrupy, about 20 minutes longer.

Remove from the heat and season with lots of pepper. Let cool to room temperature and serve. The marmalade will keep, tightly covered, in the refrigerator for up to 2 months; bring to room temperature before serving.

SHOP
AND
SERVE
ANTIPASTI

BEAUTY BY THE SLICE
# AFFETTATI

*AFFETTATO* MEANS "SLICED," and *affettati* are sliced salumi. Arrange thin slices of prosciutto, assorted salami, *coppa*, and mortadella on a large platter. Work carefully to show off how beautiful and distinctive each type is. Or, you can do as the Italians sometimes do and cut the mortadella into cubes for spearing with toothpicks. Serve the meats at room temperature with crusty bread and sweet butter. For a more substantial offering, set out a condiment or two (see pages 38 to 47) and a platter of cheeses.

# Bruschette di puré di fagioli e salame

## BRUSCHETTA WITH WHITE BEAN PUREE AND SALAME TOPPING

Here, white beans are cooked until soft, pureed, mixed with olive oil and garlic, and then spread on grilled bread and topped with salame. In the variation, the bean puree is topped with sautéed bitter greens, a popular Pugliese combination known as *n'capriata*. WINE Verdicchio, Frascati, or Sauvignon Blanc SERVES 8

1 CUP DRIED GREAT NORTHERN BEANS, SOAKED OVER-
  NIGHT IN WATER TO COVER, DRAINED, AND RINSED

6 CUPS WATER

SALT

⅓ CUP EXTRA VIRGIN OLIVE OIL

4 CLOVES GARLIC, MINCED

½ TEASPOON FRESHLY GROUND BLACK PEPPER

8 SLICES COARSE COUNTRY BREAD, GRILLED OR
  BROILED AND RUBBED ON ONE SIDE WITH A HALVED
  GARLIC CLOVE

8 SLICES SALAME, CHOPPED INTO SMALL PIECES

In a saucepan, combine the beans and water and bring to a boil over medium-high heat. Add 1 teaspoon salt, reduce heat to low, and simmer gently, uncovered, until very soft, 50 to 75 minutes. Drain the beans, reserving the liquid. You should have about 3 cups beans. In a food processor, process the beans, adding as much of the cooking liquid as necessary to form a smooth and spreadable puree. Reserve the remaining cooking liquid in case the puree thickens too much as it cools. Transfer the puree to a bowl.

In a small skillet, warm the olive oil over medium heat. Add the garlic and sauté just until softened and fragrant, 1 to 2 minutes. Add to the bean puree, season with about 1 teaspoon salt and the pepper, and mix well.

Let the bean puree cool until warm or to room temperature, adding some of the reserved liquid if necessary to achieve a good spreading consistency. (The puree can also be cooled completely, covered, and refrigerated for up to 2 days ahead. Rewarm over low heat, adding some of the reserved liquid as needed to thin.) Spread the bean puree on the garlic-rubbed side of the bread slices. Strew the salame evenly over the tops and serve at once.

*Variation with Greens and Pancetta:* Prepare the bean puree as directed, and omit the salame. Bring a large pot of salted water to a boil. Trim the tough stems from 2 pounds escarole, broccoli rabe, dandelion greens, Swiss chard, or other bitter green, and cut the greens into 1-inch-wide strips. Add to the boiling water and cook until tender, about 10 minutes. Drain, rinse under cold running water to halt the cooking and set the color, and drain again, then chop coarsely. In a large sauté pan, warm 3 tablespoons extra virgin olive oil over medium heat and add a pinch of red pepper flakes. Add ¼ pound pancetta, sliced ¼ inch thick and then cut into strips ¼ inch wide, and sauté until almost crisp, 5 to 7 minutes. Transfer to a plate and set aside. Add the greens to the fat remaining in the pan and warm through. Add 2 to 3 tablespoons red wine vinegar and cook, stirring, for 2 minutes to blend the flavors. Return the pancetta to the pan and mix well. Season to taste with salt and pepper. Top the bread slices with the bean puree and then with the warm greens. Drizzle with extra virgin olive oil and serve at once.

# Bruschette, panini e tramezzini

## BRUSCHETTE AND SANDWICHES

Most Italian sandwiches fall into two types, *panini* and *tramezzini*. The first typically calls for tucking ingredients into a soft roll, or *panino*, while the latter slips ingredients between two slices of white sandwich bread, usually with the crusts removed. Bruschetta, ingredients piled atop grilled bread (and sometimes focaccia), is a type of open-faced sandwich commonly served as an antipasto. Most of these sandwiches are served at room temperature but a few are served warm and some are toasted. Suggestions for incorporating salumi in these classic snacks and antipasti follow.

### BRUSCHETTA SUGGESTIONS

*Made with Bread:* The bread for these iconic antipasti must be crusty, flavorful, and hearty; the olive oil must be fruity; the garlic must be pungent but not bitter; and the grill or broiler must be hot enough to mark the slices evenly. Cut coarse country bread into slices about ½ inch thick, and brush on both sides with extra virgin olive oil. Grill or broil the bread until marked on both sides and slightly crisp. Immediately rub the bread on one side with the cut side of a halved garlic clove. Top the garlic-rubbed side with one of the following suggestions, layering the ingredients in the order given:

- Pear or fig slices and *coppa* or prosciutto slices.

- Light coating of fresh goat cheese, pear slices, and *coppa* slices.

- Mix Gorgonzola cheese with unsalted butter or mascarpone cheese and chopped walnuts or hazelnuts and spread on bread; top with prosciutto slices, pear or fig slices, and watercress leaves.

- Tomato slices, fresh mozzarella slices, and salame slices.

- Tomato slices, avocado slices, fresh mozzarella slices, and *coppa* slices.

- Light coating of pesto, tomato slices, fresh mozzarella slices, and *coppa* or salame slices.

- Light coating of tapenade, chopped roasted peppers, and salame slices.

*Made with Focaccia:* Most focaccia is too thick to use for sandwiches, but it is ideal for making open-faced bruschette that you slip under the broiler or warm briefly in a hot oven. Top small squares or rectangles of focaccia with one of the following suggestions, layering the ingredients in the order given:

- Salame slices and finely shredded Fontina cheese; place under broiler until cheese melts.

- Halved red grapes, salame slices, and grated Parmesan; place under broiler until cheese is bubbly and golden and grapes have given off some juice. CONTINUED ▶

- Light coating of pesto, tomato slices, salame strips, and fresh mozzarella slices; place under broiler until cheese melts.

### PANINO AND TRAMEZZINO SUGGESTIONS

Slice Frittata with Potatoes, Onion, Zucchini, and Salame (page 74); spread a soft roll with a little mayonnaise, tuck in a piece of frittata and a lettuce leaf.

Slice Frittata with Potatoes, Onion, Zucchini, and Salame (page 74); spread a soft roll with a little mayonnaise, tuck in a piece of frittata and some Sweet-and-Sour Peppers with Almonds (page 42), and drizzle with olive oil and vinegar.

Make scrambled eggs with salame; spread a soft roll with butter and tuck in the scrambled eggs and tomato slices.

Make scrambled eggs with salame, onion, and tomato; spread a soft roll with butter and tuck in the scrambled eggs.

Spread a soft roll or white sandwich bread (crusts removed) with mayonnaise mixed with a little mustard and chopped cornichons, and fill with mortadella slices and provolone slices.

Spread a soft roll or 2 slices white sandwich bread (crusts removed) with tapenade, and fill with fresh mozzarella slices and *coppa* or salame slices.

Spread a soft roll or 2 slices white sandwich bread (crusts removed) with pesto, and fill with fresh mozzarella slices, tomato slices (optional), and prosciutto or salame slices.

Layer Fontina slices and prosciutto or salame slices between 2 slices white sandwich bread (crusts removed); brush the outsides of the sandwich with unsalted butter and fry on both sides on a griddle or in a skillet, weighting the sandwich with a heavy pan, or toast in a stove-top or electric *panini* press.

# Panini al gorgonzola, pera e prosciutto

**PANINI WITH GORGONZOLA, SLICED PEAR, AND PROSCIUTTO**

These *panini* can also be made with apples in place of the pears, and salame or *coppa* in place of the prosciutto. Select a soft, creamy Gorgonzola *dolce* (sweet) for a mild flavor, or a firmer Gorgonzola *piccante* (tangy) for an earthier, sharper flavor. If you choose a hard Gorgonzola, it can be combined with the mascarpone in a food processor.   **SERVES** 4

¼ POUND GORGONZOLA CHEESE AT ROOM
  TEMPERATURE

½ POUND MASCARPONE CHEESE

½ CUP CHOPPED TOASTED WALNUTS OR HAZELNUTS

2 TABLESPOONS UNSALTED BUTTER

1 RED ONION, THINLY SLICED

2 FIRM BUT RIPE PEARS, PEELED, HALVED, CORED,
  AND SLICED

4 SANDWICH ROLLS, EACH ABOUT 5 INCHES LONG, SPLIT

12 THIN SLICES PROSCIUTTO, SALAME, OR *COPPA*

In a small bowl, mix together the Gorgonzola and mascarpone with a fork. Add the nuts and stir to distribute evenly. Set aside.

In a sauté pan, melt the butter over medium heat. Add the onion and cook, stirring occasionally, until softened, about 8 minutes. Add the pears and cook, stirring occasionally, until softened and caramelized, 8 to 10 minutes. Remove from the heat.

Spread the cheese mixture on one-half of each roll. Top with the prosciutto and then the sautéed pear mixture. Close the sandwiches and serve.

# Panini al caprino, rucola, peperoni e salame

## PANINI WITH GOAT CHEESE, ARUGULA, ROASTED PEPPERS, AND SALAME

You can omit the herbs and garlic in the cheese, but the few extra minutes it takes to mix them in are rewarded with a bolder-flavored *panino*. Or, you can save time by purchasing an herbed fresh goat's or cow's milk cheese. Any salame—hot, mild, or herbed—will complement the other ingredients. **SERVES** 4

5 OUNCES FRESH GOAT CHEESE

2 TABLESPOONS MINCED FRESH CHIVES

1 TABLESPOON CHOPPED FRESH FLAT-LEAF PARSLEY

1 CLOVE GARLIC, MINCED

4 SANDWICH ROLLS, EACH ABOUT 5 INCHES LONG, SPLIT

2 ROASTED RED BELL PEPPERS, SEEDED AND CUT
    LENGTHWISE INTO NARROW STRIPS

24 SLICES SALAME

EXTRA VIRGIN OLIVE OIL FOR DRIZZLING

SMALL HANDFUL OF ARUGULA LEAVES

In a small bowl, stir the goat cheese briefly to smooth it out. Add the chives, parsley, and garlic and mix well.

Spread the goat cheese on one-half of each roll. Top with the peppers, and then the salame. Drizzle a bit of olive oil on the other half, and top with some arugula leaves.

Close the sandwiches and serve.

# Hero Sandwich

A delicatessen classic, this popular Italian-American sandwich is aptly named: You have to be heroic to finish it. Its origin lies in the southern Italian immigrant community of late-nineteenth-century New York, where workers satisfied their noontime hunger with a taste of home. You can substitute the garlic vinaigrette on page 126 for the olive oil and vinegar.  SERVES 4

4 PIECES ITALIAN COUNTRY BREAD LOAF, EACH
    ABOUT 8 INCHES LONG

EXTRA VIRGIN OLIVE OIL FOR DRIZZLING

RED OR WHITE WINE VINEGAR FOR DRIZZLING

FRESHLY GROUND BLACK PEPPER

½ CUP GRATED PARMESAN CHEESE

8 THIN SLICES *COPPA*

8 THIN SLICES GENOA SALAME

8 THIN SLICES *SOPRESSATA*

8 THIN SLICES MORTADELLA

16 SLICES SMOKED MOZZARELLA OR SMOKED
    PROVOLONE CHEESE

12 PAPER-THIN SLICES RED ONION

32 SLICES ROASTED RED BELL PEPPER

Split the bread pieces so they open fairly flat, like a book, but don't cut all the way through. Drizzle the cut sides of all the bread pieces with olive oil and vinegar and season with pepper. Sprinkle each cut side with 1 tablespoon of the Parmesan. Layer all of the meats and the cheese slices on one-half of the bread pieces, and top each stack with 3 onion slices and 8 red pepper slices. Fold over to close the sandwiches and serve.

# Pane per la pizza

BASIC PIZZA DOUGH

You can buy ready-made pizza dough in the refrigerated section of your supermarket. But making pizza dough is easy, especially with this nearly foolproof recipe. It includes a sponge, which gives the yeast a head start. You can mix and knead the dough by hand or in a stand mixer fitted with a dough hook. MAKES one 11-by-17-inch crust or two 9-inch round crusts

SPONGE

1 TABLESPOON ACTIVE DRY YEAST

1/4 CUP LUKEWARM WATER

1/4 CUP UNBLEACHED ALL-PURPOSE FLOUR

DOUGH

3/4 CUP COOL WATER

3 TABLESPOONS OLIVE OIL

3 1/4 CUPS UNBLEACHED ALL-PURPOSE FLOUR

1 1/2 TEASPOONS SALT

YELLOW CORNMEAL FOR DUSTING PIZZA STONE

To make the sponge, in a large bowl, sprinkle the yeast over the warm water and let stand until foamy, about 5 minutes. Add the flour and stir to combine. Cover and let stand at room temperature until bubbly, 20 to 30 minutes.

To make the dough by hand, add the cool water, olive oil, flour, and salt to the sponge and stir until the mixture comes together in a dough. Turn the dough out onto a lightly floured work surface and knead until soft and smooth, about 10 minutes, then shape into a ball. To make the dough by stand mixer fitted with a dough hook, add the rest of the ingredients to the sponge and mix on low speed until the dough leaves the sides of bowl cleanly and is soft and smooth, about 10 minutes, then shape into a ball.

Transfer the dough to an oiled bowl, cover with plastic wrap, and let the dough rise in a warm spot until doubled in bulk, about 1 hour.

Lightly flour a rimmed baking sheet. Turn the dough out onto a lightly floured work surface, punch down, and then shape into a ball, or divide in half and shape into 2 balls. Place on the prepared baking sheet, cover with plastic wrap, and let rest in the refrigerator for 30 minutes. (Or, you can refrigerate the dough overnight.) Bring the dough to room temperature before you shape it.

If you have a pizza stone or quarry tiles, place on the lowest rack or on the floor of the oven (be careful you don't cover any vents in the floor), and preheat the oven to 475° to 500°F (at least 30 minutes if using a stone or tiles).

To shape the dough, transfer it to lightly floured work surface and pull, lift, and stretch it into an 11-by-17-inch rectangle or two 9-inch rounds (or roll out the dough with a rolling pin). It should be about 1/4 inch thick and slightly thinner in the middle than at the edges. Lift the edges to form a shallow rim.

If using a pizza stone or tiles, transfer the dough to a baker's peel (or an inverted baking sheet), and top as directed in individual recipes. Dust the stone or tiles with cornmeal and slide the pizza onto the stone. Or, transfer the dough to a well-seasoned large baking sheet, top as directed in individual recipes, and place on the lowest rack in the oven. Bake until the crust is golden and well puffed, 12 to 15 minutes.

# Pizza alla pancetta, porri e formaggio

## PIZZA WITH PANCETTA, LEEKS, AND GRUYÈRE CHEESE

This is a northern Italian pizza topping with a French accent, which should come as no surprise since Piedmont was long ruled by France. Gruyère cheese, which is made by both the Swiss (no holes) and the French (with holes), is popular in this part of Italy, where it is known as *groviera svizzera*.   **WINE** Dolcetto, Pinot Noir, or Pinot Bianco   **SERVES** 2 to 4

BASIC PIZZA DOUGH (FACING PAGE)

2 TABLESPOONS UNSALTED BUTTER OR 1 TABLESPOON
   EACH OLIVE OIL AND UNSALTED BUTTER

3 CUPS CHOPPED LEEKS, WHITE AND GREEN PARTS,
   WELL WASHED AND DRAINED

FRESHLY GRATED NUTMEG

SALT AND FRESHLY GROUND BLACK PEPPER

6 OUNCES PANCETTA, SLICED ¼ INCH THICK AND THEN
   CUT INTO STRIPS ¼ INCH WIDE

½ POUND GRUYÈRE CHEESE OR ¼ POUND EACH FRESH
   MOZZARELLA AND GRUYÈRE CHEESE, SHREDDED

OLIVE OIL FOR BRUSHING

3 TABLESPOONS GRATED PARMESAN CHEESE

Make the pizza dough and refrigerate as directed, then preheat the oven as directed.

In a heavy sauté pan, melt the butter over medium heat. Add the leeks and cook, stirring occasionally, until tender, about 10 minutes. Drain the cooked leeks in a sieve, transfer to a bowl, and season to taste with nutmeg, salt, and pepper.

Rinse the pan, return to medium heat, and add the pancetta. Cook the pancetta in its own rendered fat, stirring occasionally, until almost cooked through but not crisp, 5 to 7 minutes. Remove from the heat. Using a slotted spoon, transfer the pancetta to a plate.

Shape the pizza dough as directed, and sprinkle evenly with the Gruyère cheese. Top with the pancetta and then the leeks.

Bake until the crust is golden and well puffed, 12 to 15 minutes. Remove from the oven, brush the edges of the crust with olive oil, and sprinkle the Parmesan evenly over the filling. Serve at once.

# Pizza al pancetta, pomodori secchi, cipolle rosse e basilico

**PIZZA WITH PANCETTA, SUN-DRIED TOMATOES, RED ONIONS, AND BASIL**

Here, olive oil–packed sun-dried tomatoes replace the usual tomato sauce, and a little of the flavorful oil from the tomatoes is brushed over the dough before the toppings are added.  **WINE** Valpolicella, Barbera, or Chianti  **SERVES** 2 to 4

BASIC PIZZA DOUGH (PAGE 58)

6 OUNCES PANCETTA, SLICED ¼ INCH THICK AND THEN
   CUT INTO STRIPS ¼ INCH WIDE

2 RED ONIONS, CUT INTO ¼-INCH-THICK SLICES

2 TABLESPOONS OLIVE OIL

½ CUP OIL-PACKED SUN-DRIED TOMATOES, DRAINED,
   WITH OIL RESERVED, AND CUT INTO NARROW STRIPS

1 TABLESPOON MINCED GARLIC, STEEPED IN 1
   TABLESPOON EXTRA VIRGIN OLIVE OIL

3 TO 5 OUNCES FRESH MOZZARELLA CHEESE, SHREDDED

½ CUP GRATED PECORINO CHEESE

¼ CUP FINELY SHREDDED FRESH BASIL

Make the pizza dough and refrigerate as directed, then preheat the oven as directed.

In a large sauté pan, cook the pancetta in its own rendered fat over medium heat, stirring occasionally, until almost cooked through but not crisp, 5 to 7 minutes. Remove from the heat. Using a slotted spoon, transfer the pancetta to a plate and set aside.

Add the onions and the olive oil to the fat remaining in the pan and cook over medium heat, stirring occasionally, until tender, about 10 minutes. Remove from the heat.

Shape the pizza dough as directed, and brush the sun-dried tomato oil and minced garlic and its oil on the bottom of the crust. Sprinkle the mozzarella evenly over the crust, and then top with the onions and pancetta. Strew the tomato strips over the top.

Bake until the crust is golden and well puffed, 12 to 15 minutes. Remove from the oven and sprinkle with the pecorino and basil. Serve at once.

# Pizza di ricotta e salame

## RICOTTA PIE WITH POTATO CRUST

A dough made from potatoes develops a wonderfully chewy texture. Baking the potatoes, rather than boiling them, yields a crust that is a bit firmer, though it will not become fully crisp in either case. The mild potato flavor and creamy ricotta are perfect foils for the salty, meaty salame and briny olives.   WINE Pinot Bianco, Greco di Tufo, or Sauvignon Blanc   SERVES 8

2 CUPS (ABOUT 1 POUND) FRESH WHOLE-MILK
   RICOTTA CHEESE

1 POUND BOILING OR BAKING POTATOES

1 2/3 CUPS UNBLEACHED ALL-PURPOSE FLOUR,
   OR AS NEEDED

1 TEASPOON SALT

1 TABLESPOON OLIVE OIL

1/2 CUP SLICED PITTED GREEN OLIVES

1/2 CUP SLIVERED *CRESPONE* OR *SOPRESSATA*

FRESHLY GROUND BLACK PEPPER

1/4 CUP GRATED PARMESAN CHEESE

1 TABLESPOON CHOPPED FRESH MARJORAM OR
   SUMMER SAVORY

If the cheese contains a lot of moisture, spoon it into a sieve placed over a bowl and let drain for at least 1 hour at room temperature or longer in the refrigerator.

Meanwhile, preheat the oven to 400°F. Prick the potato skins in a few places with a fork, place the potatoes on a rimmed baking sheet, and bake until very soft, about 1 hour. Let the potatoes cool just until they can be handled. Then cut them in half, scoop out the flesh into a ricer or food mill, discarding the skins, and pass the flesh through the ricer or mill into a bowl. Or, scoop the flesh directly into the bowl and mash with a potato masher.

If you are short on time, peel the potatoes, cut them into chunks, and place them in a saucepan with lightly salted water to cover generously. Bring to a boil over high heat, reduce the heat to medium, and cook until tender, 20 to 30 minutes. Drain well and pass through a ricer or food mill placed over a bowl, or mash them, then proceed as directed.

Add the 1 2/3 cups flour, the salt, and the olive oil and, using a fork or wooden spoon, mix until the ingredients come together in a dough. Turn the dough out onto a lightly floured work surface and knead until a firm, smooth dough forms (similar to a dough for gnocchi), adding more flour as needed to achieve the correct consistency. (You can also mix the dough in a stand mixer fitted with the paddle attachment.)

If you have baked the potatoes, reduce the oven temperature to 375°F. If you have boiled them, preheat the oven to 375°F. Lightly oil a rimmed baking sheet.

On a lightly floured work surface, roll out or pat out the dough into an 11-inch round (or into an oval, square, or rectangle) about 1/4 inch thick. Transfer to the prepared baking sheet and fold up the edges like a pizza crust.

Spread the ricotta evenly over the potato crust, and then distribute the olives and *crespone* evenly over the ricotta. Sprinkle evenly with the pepper, Parmesan, and marjoram. Bake until the crust is golden and the filling is set, 30 to 45 minutes. Remove from the oven and place on a rack to cool slightly. Serve warm, cut into wedges.

SHOP
AND
SERVE
ANTIPASTI

## CLEAN, CRISP, AND DELICIOUS

# PINZIMONIO

SERVE *PINZIMONIO* ALONGSIDE a selection of salumi. Assemble a platter of carrot and celery sticks and fennel and pepper strips, or place vegetables in a clear-glass bowl with an inch or two of ice water. Accompany with extra virgin olive oil for dipping, and coarse sea salt for sprinkling. The clear flavors of the vegetables and oil will allow the salumi to shine.

In the United States, mustard and pickles are often served with salumi, but their sharpness can mask the flavor of high-quality cured meats. Cornichons, which are sweeter than dill pickles, are sometimes a suitable accompaniment. Avoid *giardiniera*, Italian mixed pickled vegetables, as its sharp blast of vinegar can overwhelm the delicate spices in the best salumi.

# Schiacciata

**DOUBLE-CRUSTED PIZZA**

Double-crusted pizzas are found primarily in southern and central Italy. In Puglia, Calabria, and Sicily, the double-crusted pie is sometimes called a *pitta*, a holdover from when the Greeks ruled these regions. In Tuscany, it is known as a *schiacciata*, which means "flattened" or "squashed." If you are pressed for time, you can use store-bought pizza dough. **WINE** Primitivo or Zinfandel **SERVES** 8

BASIC PIZZA DOUGH (PAGE 58)

2 CUPS (ABOUT 1 POUND) FRESH WHOLE-MILK RICOTTA CHEESE, SPOONED INTO A SIEVE AND ALLOWED TO DRAIN FOR 1 HOUR AT ROOM TEMPERATURE

½ TEASPOON SALT

¼ POUND SALAME, PEELED AND CHOPPED

2 OUNCES *RICOTTA SALATA* OR PROVOLONE CHEESE, GRATED

3 HARD-BOILED EGGS, PEELED AND CHOPPED

OLIVE OIL FOR BRUSHING

Make the pizza dough, divide into 2 balls, and refrigerate as directed, then preheat the oven as directed.

To shape the dough, transfer 1 ball to a lightly floured work surface and pull, lift, and stretch it into a round about 14 inches in diameter (or roll out the dough with a rolling pin). Repeat with the second ball to form a second round the same size. Transfer 1 dough round to a baker's peel if using a pizza stone or tiles, or to an oiled baking sheet or 14-inch pizza pan.

In a bowl, combine the ricotta and salt and mix well. Spread the fresh ricotta evenly over the round on the peel, leaving the edges uncovered. Strew the salame, the *ricotta salata*, and then the eggs evenly over the ricotta. Top with the second dough round and pinch the edges together to seal.

Brush the top with olive oil, then either slide the *schiacciata* onto the pizza stone or place the pan in the oven. Bake until golden brown, 18 to 20 minutes.

If using a pizza stone, remove the *schiacciata* from the oven with the baker's peel and slide it onto a wire rack. If using a pan, transfer the pan to the rack. Let cool for at least 15 minutes. Serve warm or at room temperature, cut into wedges.

# Crocchette di riso e salsicce

## RICE CROQUETTES WITH CRESPONE OR COTECHINO

The rice for these croquettes is started in the same way you make a risotto: You sauté it with finely chopped vegetables and sausage until it is opaque. But the liquid—broth, rather than water, for a deeper flavor—is added all at once. There is no filling, which makes the croquettes fast and easy to assemble. A sprinkle of truffle salt delivers an aromatic finish. **WINE** Prosecco, Orvieto, or Montefalco Rosso **MAKES** about 32 croquettes

2 TABLESPOONS UNSALTED BUTTER OR OLIVE OIL

½ YELLOW ONION, FINELY CHOPPED

1 CARROT, PEELED AND FINELY CHOPPED

1 CELERY STALK, FINELY CHOPPED

¼ POUND *CRESPONE* OR *COTECHINO*, CASING REMOVED AND CHOPPED

1 CUP ARBORIO, VIALONE NANO, OR OTHER SHORT-GRAIN ITALIAN RICE

2 CUPS CHICKEN BROTH

1 EGG

GRATED ZEST OF 1 LEMON

¼ CUP GRATED PARMESAN CHEESE

1 BLACK TRUFFLE, GRATED, OR 1 TABLESPOON TRUFFLE PASTE (OPTIONAL)

1 CUP ALL-PURPOSE FLOUR

1 CUP FINE DRIED BREAD CRUMBS

2 EGGS

OLIVE OIL OR EQUAL PARTS OLIVE AND CANOLA OIL FOR DEEP-FRYING

TRUFFLE SALT FOR FINISHING (OPTIONAL)

In a sauté pan, melt the butter over medium heat. Add the onion, carrot, and celery and cook, stirring occasionally, until softened, about 10 minutes. Add the sausage and stir until it colors slightly, about 8 minutes. Add the rice and stir until the rice is opaque, about 3 minutes. Pour in the broth and cook, uncovered, just until the broth is absorbed by the rice and the rice is just cooked through, 10 to 15 minutes. Remove from the heat and let cool for about 5 minutes. The rice will continue to soften as it sits.

Add the egg, lemon zest, cheese, and grated truffle to the rice and stir to mix well. Spoon the rice out onto a rimmed baking sheet, spreading it evenly so that it cools quickly. Refrigerate until fully cooled but not hard, 1 to 2 hours.

To shape the croquettes, line 2 large rimmed baking sheets with parchment paper. Dampen your hands with water. Scoop up a spoonful of the rice, shape into a ball 1 ½ inches in diameter, and place on a parchment-lined baking sheet. Repeat until all the rice is used, continuing to dampen your hands as you work so the rice does not stick to your fingers. CONTINUED ▸

Pour the flour and bread crumbs into separate shallow bowls. In a third shallow bowl, lightly beat the eggs just until blended. One at a time, dip the croquettes in the flour, then in the eggs, and finally in the bread crumbs, coating evenly each time, and place on the second prepared baking sheet. You can fry the croquettes right away, or cover and refrigerate for at least 1 hour or up to 24 hours. Even a short stint in the refrigerator firms them up, making them easier to fry.

Preheat the oven to 200°F. Line a large ovenproof tray with paper towels. Pour oil to a depth of 2 inches into a heavy saucepan and heat to 360°F on a deep-frying thermometer. Place a few croquettes on a wire skimmer, slip them into the hot oil, and fry until golden brown, 3 to 4 minutes. Using the wire skimmer, transfer the croquettes to the towel-lined tray to drain and keep warm in the oven for up to 15 minutes. Repeat until all the croquettes are cooked.

Arrange the croquettes on a warmed platter, and sprinkle with the truffle salt. Serve this finger food piping hot with a stack of napkins.

# Supplì al telefono

RICE CROQUETTES, ROMAN STYLE

In Italy, rice croquettes come in many shapes and sizes: flattened cakes; small balls; big balls (called *arancine*, or "little oranges"); good-sized pyramids; and football shaped. They are usually stuffed with cheese, vegetables, and/or meats, and the rice may be tinted with saffron or not. These classic croquettes, a Roman specialty whose name translates as "telephone wires," are stuffed with a mixture of prosciutto, porcini mushrooms, tomato paste, and mozzarella. Their name comes from what happens when you eat them: When you bite into one and draw it away from your mouth, the melted cheese forms stringlike strands reminiscent of telephone cords. While the croquettes can be mixed, shaped, and refrigerated well ahead of time, you must fry them just before serving.   WINE Prosecco or Franciacorta   MAKES 12 to 16 croquettes

**RICE MIXTURE**

3 1/2 CUPS WATER

1 1/2 TEASPOONS SALT

2 CUPS ARBORIO RICE

2 EGGS

2/3 CUP GRATED PARMESAN CHEESE

1/4 TEASPOON FRESHLY GROUND BLACK PEPPER

**FILLING**

2 TABLESPOONS OLIVE OIL

1/2 CUP CHOPPED YELLOW ONION

1 TEASPOON FINELY MINCED GARLIC

2 TABLESPOONS DRIED PORCINI MUSHROOMS, SOAKED
    IN 1/3 CUP HOT WATER FOR 30 MINUTES, DRAINED,
    WITH LIQUID RESERVED, AND FINELY CHOPPED
    (ABOUT 1/4 CUP CHOPPED)

1/4 CUP DICED PROSCIUTTO

2 TEASPOONS TOMATO PASTE, DILUTED IN 1
    TABLESPOON WARM WATER

SALT AND FRESHLY GROUND BLACK PEPPER

1/2 POUND FRESH MOZZARELLA CHEESE, CUT INTO
    3/4-INCH CUBES

1 CUP ALL-PURPOSE FLOUR

1 CUP FINE DRIED BREAD CRUMBS

2 EGGS

OLIVE OIL OR EQUAL PARTS OLIVE AND CANOLA OIL
    FOR DEEP-FRYING

To make the rice mixture, in a saucepan, combine the water and 1 teaspoon of the salt and bring to a boil over high heat. Add the rice, stir well, reduce the heat to low, cover, and cook until the liquid is absorbed and the rice is cooked through but still sticky, about 15 minutes. Remove from the heat and let cool for 5 minutes.

Add the eggs, cheese, the remaining 1/2 teaspoon salt, and the pepper to the rice and mix well. Spoon the rice out onto a rimmed baking sheet, spreading it evenly. Refrigerate until cooled but not hard, 1 to 2 hours.   CONTINUED ▶

Meanwhile, make the filling. In a sauté pan, warm the olive oil over medium heat. Add the onion and sauté until soft and translucent, 8 to 10 minutes. Add the garlic, porcini and their soaking liquid, prosciutto, and tomato paste, stir well, and simmer, stirring occasionally, until the mixture is thick, about 15 minutes. Season to taste with salt and pepper. Transfer to a bowl and let cool completely. Have the mozzarella ready.

To shape and stuff the croquettes, line 2 large rimmed baking sheets with parchment paper. Dampen your hands with water. Scoop up a spoonful of the rice and shape into an oval about 2 ½ inches long and 1 ½ inches in diameter. With an index finger, make an indentation in the rice. Spoon some of the filling into the center, and then tuck in a cube of mozzarella. Smooth the rice over the filling, reshaping the croquette, and place on a parchment-lined baking sheet. Repeat until all the rice is used, continuing to dampen your hands as you work so the rice does not stick to your fingers.

Pour the flour and bread crumbs into separate shallow bowls. In a third shallow bowl, lightly beat the eggs just until blended. One at a time, dip the croquettes in the flour, then in the eggs, and finally in the bread crumbs, coating evenly each time, and place on the second prepared baking sheet. Cover and refrigerate until fully chilled, at least 2 hours or up to 24 hours. Even a short stint in the refrigerator firms them up, making them easier to fry.

Preheat the oven to 200°F. Line an ovenproof tray with paper towels. Pour oil to a depth of 3 inches into a heavy saucepan and heat to 350°F on a deep-frying thermometer. Place a few croquettes on a wire skimmer, slip them into the hot oil, and fry until golden brown, 6 to 7 minutes. As the croquettes fry, lift them out of the hot oil with the wire skimmer, hold them for a minute, and then slip them back into the hot oil. Repeat this process twice. If you do not do this, the croquettes will be golden on the outside but the mozzarella will remain solid and cool. Using the wire skimmer, transfer the croquettes to the towel-lined tray to drain and keep warm in the oven for up to 15 minutes. Repeat until all the croquettes are cooked.

Arrange the croquettes on a warmed platter and serve piping hot. This is finger food, so don't forget the napkins.

# Rotolone d'uovo

## SALUMI-FILLED OMELET ROLL

You will need a good-sized sauté pan for this dish because the omelet must be large enough to stuff and roll easily. The roll can be prepared up to a day in advance and refrigerated. Slice the chilled roll and then let the slices come to room temperature before serving.   **WINE** Verdicchio or Fiano d'Avellino   **SERVES** 8

**OMELET**

6 EGGS

1 TABLESPOON ALL-PURPOSE FLOUR

3 TABLESPOONS GRATED PARMESAN CHEESE

2 TABLESPOONS WHOLE MILK

2 TABLESPOONS MINCED FRESH CHIVES

2 TEASPOONS SALT

2 TABLESPOONS UNSALTED BUTTER, OR AS NEEDED

**FILLING**

¼ CUP MAYONNAISE

1 ROUNDED TABLESPOON DIJON MUSTARD

2 TABLESPOONS CHOPPED CORNICHON (OPTIONAL)

3 OUNCES THINLY SLICED PROSCIUTTO

3 OUNCES THINLY SLICED MORTADELLA

To make the omelet, in a bowl, whisk together the eggs, flour, cheese, milk, chives, and salt until well blended.

In a 12-inch sauté pan, melt the 2 tablespoons butter over medium heat. When the butter begins to foam, pour in the egg mixture and cook until golden on the underside and barely set on top, 3 to 4 minutes. Invert a platter or pizza pan slightly larger than the sauté pan over the pan and, holding the pan and platter together, flip them. Lift off the sauté pan and return it to medium heat. If the pan looks dry, add a little more butter and allow it to melt until foaming. Slide the omelet,

browned side up, back into the pan and cook just long enough to set fully on the second side, 2 to 3 minutes. Remove from the heat. (If you are not sure you are agile enough to flip the omelet successfully, you can cook as directed on the first side, slip the pan—make sure it is flameproof—under a preheated broiler for a few minutes, or into a preheated 350°F oven for 10 minutes, to set the top.)

Lay a dish towel on a work surface and slide the finished omelet onto it. Let cool for about 10 minutes. The paler side (the side that was cooked first) should be facing up.

To make the filling, in a small bowl, stir together the mayonnaise, mustard, and cornichon. Spread two-thirds of the mayonnaise mixture evenly over the surface of the omelet. Top evenly, first with the prosciutto slices and then the mortadella slices. Spread the mortadella with the remaining mayonnaise mixture. Working carefully, roll up the omelet into a compact cylinder and place, seam side down, on a sheet of plastic wrap. Enclose the roll in the plastic wrap and then in aluminum foil. Chill for at least 4 hours or overnight before serving.

To serve, cut the chilled omelet roll crosswise into 1-inch-thick slices (each one is a perfect mouthful) and arrange on a platter. Serve at room temperature.

# Frittata con patate, cipolle, zucchini e salame

## FRITTATA WITH POTATOES, ONION, ZUCCHINI, AND SALAME

Here, the potatoes are boiled and diced before they are sautéed. That means they require much less oil than if you sauté them raw, plus the frittata is faster to prepare.

**WINE** Sauvignon Blanc or Merlot     **SERVES** 6

½ CUP OLIVE OIL

ABOUT 1 POUND YUKON GOLD OR OTHER BOILING
    POTATOES, BOILED UNTIL JUST TENDER, DRAINED,
    PEELED, AND DICED (1 ½ TO 1 ¾ CUPS)

SALT AND FRESHLY GROUND BLACK PEPPER

1 YELLOW ONION, CHOPPED (ABOUT ½ CUP AFTER
    COOKING)

1 SMALL ZUCCHINI, TRIMMED AND DICED (ABOUT ½ CUP)

8 EGGS, LIGHTLY BEATEN

¼ CUP CHOPPED SALAME, PROSCIUTTO, OR *COPPA*

1 ROASTED RED BELL PEPPER, DICED (ABOUT ¼ CUP)

¼ CUP GRATED PARMESAN CHEESE

2 TABLESPOONS CHOPPED FRESH FLAT-LEAF PARSLEY

In a 10-inch skillet, warm the olive oil over medium heat. Add the potatoes, sprinkle with salt and pepper, and sauté until lightly colored and tender, 8 to 10 minutes. Using a slotted spoon, transfer to a plate and set aside.

Transfer about 2 tablespoons of the oil remaining in the pan to a small skillet, and pour the remaining oil into a measuring cup and reserve. Place the small skillet over medium heat, add the onion, and cook, stirring, until soft and pale gold, 10 to 12 minutes. Using the slotted spoon, transfer the onion to the plate holding the potatoes.

Add the zucchini to the oil remaining in the pan and cook over medium heat, stirring occasionally, until

tender, 3 to 5 minutes. Remove from the heat, add the zucchini to the plate holding the potatoes, and let cool for a few minutes. Reserve the pan.

In a bowl, whisk the eggs until blended. Mix in the potatoes, onion, and zucchini, and season lightly with salt. Add the salame, roasted pepper, and cheese and mix well.

Return the skillet to medium-high heat and add ¼ cup of the reserved olive oil. When the oil is very hot, pour in the egg mixture. Let the eggs set, shaking the pan from time to time to make sure they are not sticking, 3 to 5 minutes. Cover, reduce the heat to low, and cook until the bottom of the frittata is set and golden, about 8 minutes. Invert a platter or pizza pan slightly larger than the skillet over the pan and, holding the pan and platter together, flip them. Lift off the pan and return it to medium heat. If the pan looks dry, add a little more of the reserved oil. Slide the frittata back into the pan and cook just long enough to set the second side, 3 to 4 minutes. (If you are not sure you are agile enough to flip the frittata successfully, you can cook as directed on the first side and then slip the pan—make sure it is ovenproof—into a preheated 400°F oven for 8 minutes, to set the top.)

Slide the frittata out onto a serving plate. Sprinkle with the parsley and serve warm or at room temperature, cut into wedges.

# Primi

## FIRST COURSES

IN ITALY, A SOUP, PASTA, or grain dish is traditionally served as a *primo piatto*, or first course, in small portions. It follows a light antipasto and leads to the *secondo piatto*, or main course. Nowadays, as fewer Italians have the time to prepare or enjoy multicourse repasts, classic *primi* are sometimes served in larger portions as satisfying main courses. Because of this trend, the recipes in this chapter include servings sized for both smaller first-course and larger main-course portions.

In the soup recipes, salumi usually appear as part of the *battuto* or *soffritto*, the chopped vegetable mixture that makes up a soup's flavor base. All of the soups are good make-ahead options for busy cooks, as they can be cooked a day or two in advance and then reheated just before serving. If they include pasta or *farro*, cook it separately and add it just before serving so that it doesn't

soften too much when the soup is stored. And while you may not usually serve wine with a bowl of soup, these soups are so substantial, especially when served as a main course, that they merit a wine accompaniment.

The pasta, polenta, and rice recipes in this chapter all use salumi in much the same way they are used in soups: to enrich the dish, rather than to star in it. These additions make the dishes both more flavorful and more filling. In the United States, pasta is almost always eaten as a main course, with a pound of pasta serving four to six diners. But here you will discover the classic Italian way to serve it, too, in smaller portions, with a pound of pasta serving six to eight. ◉

# Minestrone

## MINESTRONE SOUP

Minestrone (literally "big soup") typically includes carrots, green beans, shelling beans, zucchini, potatoes, tomatoes, and pasta, but the choice of vegetables and how much of each is added is up to the cook. Chopped pancetta, prosciutto, or salame is often sautéed along with the finely chopped aromatic vegetables that form the flavor base of the soup. A loaf of good bread and a light- to medium-bodied red wine are all you need to complete the menu. **WINE** Dolcetto, Barbera, or Sangiovese  **SERVES** 12 as a first course or 8 as a main course

¼ CUP PURE OLIVE OIL

2 OUNCES PANCETTA, CUT INTO ¼-INCH DICE

2 OUNCES SALAME, PEELED AND CUT INTO ¼-INCH DICE

3 SMALL OR 2 LARGE YELLOW ONIONS, CHOPPED

5 CARROTS, PEELED AND SLICED

4 CELERY STALKS, CHOPPED

1 POUND TOMATOES, PEELED, SEEDED, AND CHOPPED

8 CUPS WATER OR CHICKEN BROTH, OR AS NEEDED

6 SMALL RED, WHITE, YUKON GOLD, OR FINGERLING POTATOES, UNPEELED, CUBED

1 CUP FRESH SHELLING BEANS, SUCH AS CRANBERRY OR LIMA; ½ CUP DRIED *CANNELLINI* OR *BORLOTTI* BEANS, SOAKED OVERNIGHT IN WATER TO COVER, DRAINED, RINSED, AND COOKED UNTIL TENDER; OR 1 CUP DRAINED, CANNED *CANNELLINI* OR *BORLOTTI* BEANS, WELL RINSED

½ POUND GREEN BEANS, TRIMMED AND CUT INTO 1-INCH LENGTHS

4 SMALL ZUCCHINI, HALVED LENGTHWISE AND THEN SLICED CROSSWISE ½ INCH THICK

4 CUPS SLICED SWISS CHARD (½-INCH-WIDE STRIPS)

1 CUP MACARONI OR SMALL PASTA SHELLS

SALT AND FRESHLY GROUND BLACK PEPPER

½ CUP BASIL PESTO (OPTIONAL)

EXTRA VIRGIN OLIVE OIL FOR FINISHING (OPTIONAL)

GRATED PARMESAN CHEESE FOR FINISHING (OPTIONAL)

In a large soup kettle, warm the pure olive oil over medium heat. Add the pancetta, salame, and onions and cook, stirring occasionally, until the onions are softened and translucent, 8 to 10 minutes. Add the carrots and celery and cook for a few minutes to soften. Add the tomatoes and 8 cups water, bring to a simmer, and simmer, uncovered, for 10 minutes to blend the flavors.

Add the potatoes and shelling beans and continue to simmer until both are tender, about 20 minutes. If using cooked dried or canned beans instead of fresh shelling beans, add them along with the green beans, zucchini, chard, and pasta during the last 10 to 15 minutes of cooking. If the vegetables and pasta are not fully covered with liquid, add water as needed to cover. (Alternatively, cook the pasta separately in salted boiling water, drain, and add to the soup just before serving.)

Season to taste with salt and pepper and remove from the heat. Stir in the pesto, and then ladle into warmed bowls. Or, remove from the heat, ladle into warmed bowls, and top each serving with a generous swirl of extra virgin olive oil and a sprinkle of Parmesan. Serve at once.

# Le virtù

## FARRO AND BEAN SOUP FROM ABRUZZO

This is an abbreviated version of a traditional—and highly complex—Abruzzese soup known as *le virtù* (the virtue), which combines seven beans, seven vegetables, and seven cuts of meat. But few of us are "virtuous" enough today to assemble and cook that many ingredients. Here is a simplified version that's just as delicious.   **WINE** Montepulciano d'Abruzzo   **SERVES** 10 as a first course or 6 to 8 as a main course

2 TO 2 ½ CUPS ASSORTED DRIED BEANS SUCH
   AS CHICKPEAS, *CANNELLINI, BORLOTTI*, AND
   LENTILS, RINSED

¼ CUP PURE OLIVE OIL

½ CUP CHOPPED PANCETTA OR PROSCIUTTO

1 LARGE YELLOW ONION, CHOPPED

2 CARROTS, PEELED AND CHOPPED

2 CELERY STALKS, CHOPPED

4 LARGE CLOVES GARLIC, MINCED

1 TABLESPOON CHOPPED FRESH SAGE

1 TABLESPOON CHOPPED FRESH MARJORAM

1 TABLESPOON CHOPPED FRESH THYME

1 ½ CUPS DICED CANNED PLUM TOMATOES

8 CUPS WATER OR CHICKEN BROTH, OR AS NEEDED

SALT AND FRESHLY GROUND BLACK PEPPER

¾ CUP *FARRO*

EXTRA VIRGIN OLIVE OIL FOR FINISHING

GRATED PARMESAN CHEESE FOR FINISHING

Soak all of the beans except the lentils overnight in water to cover, then drain. In a soup kettle, warm the pure olive oil over medium heat. Add the pancetta and cook, stirring often, until it renders its fat and is golden, about 5 minutes. Add the onion, carrots, celery, garlic, and all of the chopped herbs and cook, stirring often, until the vegetables begin to soften, about 5 minutes.

Add the drained beans and lentils, tomatoes, 8 cups water, and 2 teaspoons salt, raise the heat to high, and bring to a boil. Reduce the heat to low, cover, and simmer until all of the beans are tender, about 1 hour, checking from time to time and adding more water as needed to keep all of the ingredients covered. Season to taste with salt and pepper. (If you want a creamier soup, scoop out 1 cup of the bean mixture, puree it in a blender or food processor, and return it to the pot.)

Meanwhile, bring a saucepan filled with salted water to a boil over high heat. Add the *farro*, reduce the heat to medium, and cook until al dente, 25 to 30 minutes. Drain and add to the beans when they are tender.

Simmer the beans and *farro* together for 10 to 15 minutes, stirring often to prevent scorching. Ladle into warmed bowls and top each serving with a generous swirl of extra virgin olive oil, a sprinkle of Parmesan, and a liberal dusting of pepper. Serve at once.

# Pasta e fagioli

## PASTA AND BEANS IN BROTH

*Pasta e fagioli*, affectionately called "pasta fazool" by many Italian Americans, is made primarily in Campania and points south. It is a bowl of pasta and beans and the mixture can be brothy or quite thick, depending on the cook's preference. It can be made ahead of time and reheated, but the pasta tends to become mushy as it sits in the broth. If you prefer your pasta al dente, prepare the dish up to the point at which the pasta is added, and then add freshly cooked pasta when you reheat the beans.   WINE Sangiovese or Barbera   SERVES 10 as a first course or 6 as a main course

3 TABLESPOONS PURE OLIVE OIL

3 TO 4 OUNCES PANCETTA, CHOPPED

1 YELLOW ONION, CHOPPED

2 CARROTS, PEELED AND CHOPPED

2 CELERY STALKS, CHOPPED

3 LARGE CLOVES GARLIC, MINCED

2 CUPS (ABOUT 14 OUNCES) DRIED CRANBERRY, *BORLOTTI*, OR *CANNELLINI* OR OTHER SMALL WHITE BEANS, SOAKED OVERNIGHT IN WATER TO COVER, DRAINED, AND RINSED

1 ½ CUPS DICED CANNED PLUM TOMATOES, WITH JUICES

8 CUPS WATER OR CHICKEN BROTH, OR AS NEEDED

SALT AND FRESHLY GROUND BLACK PEPPER

½ POUND SMALL SHELLS, *DITALINI*, OR OTHER SMALL PASTA SHAPE

EXTRA VIRGIN OLIVE OIL FOR FINISHING

GRATED PARMESAN CHEESE FOR FINISHING

In a large soup kettle, warm the pure olive oil over medium heat. Add the pancetta and cook, stirring occasionally, until it renders its fat and is golden, about 5 minutes. Add the onion, carrots, celery, and garlic and cook, stirring often, until the vegetables have softened, about 5 minutes. Add the soaked beans, the tomatoes and their juices, the 8 cups water, and 2 teaspoons salt and bring to a boil. Reduce the heat to low, cover, and simmer until the beans are tender, about 1 hour.

To give the soup more body, remove 2 or 3 large spoonfuls of beans and vegetables, place in a food processor or blender, and puree until smooth. Return the puree to the pot. Taste and adjust the seasoning with salt and pepper.

Although you can cook the pasta directly in the soup, there is a danger of the soup scorching if the beans have been pureed. To avoid this, bring a large pot of salted water to a boil, add the pasta, stir well, and cook until al dente, according to the package directions. Drain the pasta, add to the soup, and simmer for 5 minutes to blend the flavors.

Ladle the soup into warmed bowls and top each serving with a generous swirl of extra virgin olive oil, a sprinkle of Parmesan, and a liberal dusting of black pepper. Serve at once.

# Zuppa di ceci e verdure

## CHICKPEA SOUP WITH GREENS

Beans and greens are such a common combination in the Italian kitchen that it is difficult to attribute this soup to a specific region. Plus, there are countless regional variations, including the beans left whole, the beans pureed, and some of the beans pureed and the remainder left whole. **WINE** Barbera, Vermentino, or Vernaccia

**SERVES** 8 as a first course or 6 as a main course

2 CUPS DRIED CHICKPEAS, SOAKED OVERNIGHT IN
    WATER TO COVER, DRAINED, AND RINSED

5 CLOVES GARLIC, 2 LEFT WHOLE AND 3 FINELY MINCED

2 LARGE YELLOW ONIONS, CHOPPED

1/3 POUND PANCETTA OR PROSCIUTTO ENDS

SALT

1/4 CUP EXTRA VIRGIN OLIVE OIL, PLUS MORE
    FOR FINISHING

4 CUPS COARSELY CHOPPED ESCAROLE OR SWISS
    CHARD (1-INCH-WIDE PIECES)

1/2 CUP SMALL PASTA SHELLS

FRESHLY GROUND BLACK PEPPER

GRATED PECORINO OR PARMESAN CHEESE FOR FINISHING

In a large saucepan, combine the soaked chickpeas, 2 whole garlic cloves, 1 chopped onion, and the pancetta pieces. Add water to cover (10 to 12 cups) and bring to a boil over high heat, skimming off any foam that forms on the surface. Add a little salt, reduce the heat to low, and cook, uncovered, until the chickpeas are just tender, about 1 hour.

Remove about 1 1/2 cups of the chickpeas from the pan and set them aside. Continue to simmer the remaining chickpeas until they are very soft, about 1 1/2 hours longer. Remove from the heat and let cool slightly. Then, working in batches, transfer the chickpeas and their

liquid—and the pancetta, if you like—to a blender and process until a smooth puree forms. Set the puree aside.

In a large saucepan, warm the 1/4 cup olive oil over medium heat. Add the remaining chopped onion, reduce the heat to low, and cook, stirring occasionally, until softened and translucent, about 10 minutes. Add the minced garlic and cook, stirring, for a minute or two. Add the escarole and stir until the greens wilt and are somewhat tender, 10 to 15 minutes.

Meanwhile, bring a saucepan filled with water to a boil, salt lightly, add the pasta, stir well, and cook until al dente, according to the package directions.

When the greens are ready, add the pureed soup base and the reserved whole chickpeas, stir well, and heat gently, stirring constantly to prevent scorching, over medium-low heat to serving temperature (adding water to thin if necessary). Taste and adjust the seasoning with salt and pepper. The soup should be peppery, but you may not need much salt because of the pancetta.

When the pasta is ready, drain well and add to the hot soup. Ladle the soup into warmed bowls and top each serving with a generous swirl of olive oil and a sprinkle of pecorino. Serve at once.

# SHOP
# AND
# SERVE
## ANTIPASTI

DRESSING UP YOUR FAVORITES

# WRAPS

SALUMI WRAPPED AROUND CHEESE, vegetables, and other complementary foods is an easy antipasto. Some simple suggestions:

- Wrap prosciutto slices around bread sticks.

- Wrap prosciutto slices around strips of provolone or fresh mozzarella cheese.

- Wrap prosciutto slices around crisp-cooked asparagus spears and serve warm or at room temperature with a shower of grated Parmesan and a drizzle of extra virgin olive oil.

- Wrap pancetta slices around figs and broil or grill.

# Spaghetti alla carbonara

## SPAGHETTI WITH PANCETTA AND EGGS

This is the quintessential Roman pasta. Cooks commonly disagree about the amount of black pepper, the proper ratio of pancetta (Romans actually prefer *guanciale*, cured pig's cheek, which is hard to find in the United States) and whether it should be allowed to crisp, or if the cheese should be Parmesan only or part Parmesan and part pecorino. No matter what they decide, the pasta will be delicious. True carbonara contains only pancetta, eggs, and cheese—no cream. Because our supermarket eggs do not have the flavor or color of the golden yolks of Roman eggs, you can add an extra yolk to the mixture.   **WINE** Dolcetto, Valpolicella, Trebbiano, or Frascati   **SERVES** 8 as a first course or 6 as a main course

3/4 POUND PANCETTA, CUT INTO 1/4-INCH-THICK SLICES

2 TABLESPOONS SALT

1 POUND SPAGHETTI

3 WHOLE EGGS PLUS 2 EGG YOLKS

6 TABLESPOONS GRATED PECORINO CHEESE, OR AS NEEDED

6 TABLESPOONS GRATED PARMESAN CHEESE, OR AS NEEDED

2 TEASPOONS FRESHLY GROUND BLACK PEPPER, OR AS NEEDED

4 TEASPOONS UNSALTED BUTTER

4 TEASPOONS OLIVE OIL

Unroll each pancetta slice and cut it crosswise into 1/4-inch-wide pieces. Set aside.

Bring a large pot filled with water to a boil. Drop in the salt and then the pasta, stir well, and cook until al dente, according to package directions.

Meanwhile, in a large bowl, whisk together the whole eggs and egg yolks, 6 tablespoons each of the cheeses, and 2 teaspoons pepper. Place the bowl near the stove or on a warming shelf.

In a sauté pan, melt the butter with the olive oil over medium heat. Add the pancetta and cook, stirring occasionally, until a layer of bubbles appears in the pan, about 7 minutes. The pancetta will be cooked but not crisp.

When the pasta is al dente, drain it and add it to the egg mixture. Immediately add the hot pancetta and most of the drippings, and toss very quickly to combine. The sauce should be a thick, creamy liquid. Taste and add more cheese and pepper, if desired.

Divide immediately among warmed pasta bowls and serve at once. This pasta does not reheat so make just enough.

*Variation with Vegetables:* Although it is not authentic, you can add a vegetable to lighten this very rich pasta. Cook 1/2 cup shelled peas, a small handful of broccoli florets, or 1/2 cup cut-up asparagus (1-inch pieces) in boiling salted water until tender yet still quite firm. Drain, refresh under cold running water to halt the cooking and set the color, and drain again. When the pasta is a minute or two away from being al dente, drop the vegetable into the pasta pot to warm through briefly. Drain the pasta and vegetables and proceed as directed.

# Bucatini all'amatriciana

## BUCATINI WITH TOMATOES, ONIONS, AND PANCETTA

This dish is named after the town of Amatrice in northeastern Lazio, near the border with Abruzzo. That geography accounts for the use of the chile here, a popular ingredient in Abruzzese dishes. The sauce, which can be prepared a little ahead of time and reheated before tossing it with the noodles, is usually paired with *bucatini* (rod pasta slightly thicker than spaghetti and with a hole), but you can also use penne or even rigatoni. **WINE** Montepulciano d'Abruzzo, Sangiovese, or Cabernet Sauvignon **SERVES** 8 as a first course or 5 or 6 as a main course

¼ CUP OLIVE OIL

½ POUND PANCETTA, SLICED ¼ INCH THICK AND CUT
    INTO STRIPS ¼ INCH WIDE

1 LARGE OR 2 MEDIUM YELLOW ONIONS, SLICED
    OR CHOPPED

1 SMALL FRESH HOT RED CHILE, CUT INTO PIECES,
    OR 1 TEASPOON RED PEPPER FLAKES

6 LARGE TOMATOES, PEELED, SEEDED, AND CHOPPED,
    OR 3 CUPS DRAINED, SEEDED, AND CHOPPED
    CANNED PLUM TOMATOES

SALT AND FRESHLY GROUND BLACK PEPPER

1 POUND PENNE OR OTHER DRIED PASTA

⅓ CUP GRATED PECORINO ROMANO CHEESE

In a large sauté pan, warm the olive oil over medium heat. Add the pancetta and cook, stirring occasionally, until it renders its fat and takes on some color but is not crisp, about 5 minutes. Using a slotted spoon, transfer the pancetta to a small bowl and set aside.

Add the onion and chile to the fat in the pan and cook over medium heat, stirring occasionally, until the onion is softened and translucent, about 8 minutes. Add the tomatoes and cook, stirring occasionally, until the sauce has thickened, about 8 minutes.

Meanwhile, bring a large pot filled with water to a boil. Drop in 2 tablespoons salt and then the pasta, stir well, and cook until al dente, according to the package directions.

When ready to serve, return the pancetta to the sauce and heat through. Season to taste with salt and pepper.

Drain the pasta and transfer to a warmed bowl. Add the sauce and toss well. Divide among warmed pasta bowls and sprinkle with the pecorino, dividing it evenly. Serve at once.

# Pasta al forno ai tre formaggi e mortadella

MACARONI WITH THREE CHEESES, MORTADELLA, AND VEGETABLES

American cooks have a way of taking a classic dish from another culture and making it their own. Macaroni and cheese, comfort food at its best, is based on the Italian classic *pasta ai tre formaggi* (pasta with three cheeses). **WINE** Barolo or Barbaresco **SERVES** 6 as a first course or 4 as a main course

**TOASTED BREAD CRUMBS**

2 THICK SLICES COARSE COUNTRY BREAD, CRUSTS REMOVED AND CUT INTO 1-INCH CUBES (1 TO 1 1/2 CUPS)

4 TABLESPOONS UNSALTED BUTTER, MELTED, OR OLIVE OIL

1/2 TEASPOON SALT

1/4 TEASPOON FRESHLY GROUND BLACK PEPPER

SALT

3/4 POUND MACARONI

1 TO 2 TABLESPOONS OLIVE OIL

1/2 CUP UNSALTED BUTTER

1/4 CUP ALL-PURPOSE FLOUR

2 CUPS WHOLE MILK

1/2 CUP HEAVY CREAM

FRESHLY GROUND BLACK PEPPER

FRESHLY GRATED NUTMEG

1/2 CUP SHREDDED FONTINA OR EMMENTALER CHEESE

1/2 CUP SHREDDED WHITE CHEDDAR CHEESE

3/4 CUP GRATED PARMESAN CHEESE

1 1/2 CUPS DICED MORTADELLA

1 CUP COOKED SHELLED PEAS AND 1 TABLESPOON MINCED FRESH CHIVES, 1 CUP COOKED BROCCOLI FLORETS, OR 1 CUP SAUTÉED MUSHROOMS

To make the toasted bread crumbs, preheat the oven to 350°F. In a food processor, pulse the bread cubes until fine crumbs form. Transfer the crumbs to a bowl, drizzle on the butter, and sprinkle with the salt and pepper. Toss well to coat evenly. Spread the bread crumbs on a rimmed baking sheet and bake, stirring occasionally, until the crumbs are golden, about 20 minutes. Let cool completely. You should have about 1 cup. (The toasted crumbs will keep in a covered container at room temperature for up to 5 days.)

Raise the oven temperature to 400°F. Butter 4 individual gratin dishes or one 9-by-12-inch baking dish.

Bring a large pot filled with water to a boil. Drop in 2 tablespoons salt and then the pasta, stir well, and cook until al dente, according to the package directions. Drain and then rinse under cold running water to halt the cooking. Transfer to a bowl, toss with the olive oil, coating well, and set aside. CONTINUED ▶

In a saucepan, melt 4 tablespoons of the butter over medium heat. Stir in the flour and cook, stirring often, until smooth, about 3 minutes. Gradually add the milk and cream while stirring constantly, then bring to a boil. Reduce the heat to low and simmer, stirring occasionally, until thickened, about 5 minutes. Remove from the heat and season to taste with salt, pepper, and nutmeg.

Add the sauce to the drained macaroni and then fold in the Fontina, Cheddar, ½ cup of the Parmesan, the mortadella, and the peas and chives. Divide among the prepared gratin dishes or spoon into the single prepared dish. Sprinkle the remaining ¼ cup Parmesan and the bread crumbs evenly over the top(s). Cut the remaining 4 tablespoons butter into small pieces and dot the top(s) evenly. (The casserole can be covered and refrigerated for up to 2 days before continuing.)

Bake until bubbly and golden brown, about 25 minutes for the small dishes and up to 35 minutes for the large dish. Let cool for about 10 minutes before serving.

# Pappardelle con fegatini di pollo

## WIDE NOODLES WITH CHICKEN LIVERS

Chicken livers make this pasta rich and creamy, while the pancetta adds a mild spiciness and a bit more richness. If you are using dried pasta, you can drop it in the water about 12 minutes before you are ready to eat. Fresh pasta takes only a few minutes to cook, so you need to make the sauce, and then cook the noodles. **WINE** Chianti or Rosso di Montalcino

**SERVES** 6 as a first course or 4 as a main course

1 POUND CHICKEN LIVERS

6 TABLESPOONS OLIVE OIL

2 CUPS SLICED FRESH MUSHROOMS SUCH AS WHITE, CREMINI, AND/OR PORCINI

3/4 POUND FRESH OR DRIED *PAPPARDELLE* OR DRIED RIGATONI

SALT

1/2 CUP DICED PANCETTA OR PROSCIUTTO

1 LARGE RED ONION, CUT INTO 1/4-INCH-THICK SLICES

6 FRESH SAGE LEAVES

2 TABLESPOONS UNSALTED BUTTER

FRESHLY GROUND BLACK PEPPER

1/2 CUP CHICKEN BROTH

1/4 CUP DRY MARSALA OR DRY WHITE WINE

2 TABLESPOONS TOMATO PASTE, DILUTED IN A LITTLE PASTA WATER (OPTIONAL)

Trim all of the fat and connective tissue from the livers, then cut away any greenish spots and separate the lobes.

In a large sauté pan, warm 2 tablespoons of the olive oil over medium heat. Add the mushrooms and cook, stirring occasionally, until slightly wilted, 3 to 5 minutes. Transfer to a plate and set aside.

Bring a large pot filled with water to a boil. If using dried pasta, add 1 tablespoon salt and then the pasta, stir well, and cook until al dente, according to the package directions. If using fresh pasta, add the salt and pasta when the sauce is almost done and cook until tender.

In the same sauté pan, warm 2 tablespoons of the olive oil over high heat. Add the pancetta (if using prosciutto, add it later), onion, and sage leaves and sauté, stirring often, until the onion is softened and golden, about 8 minutes. Transfer to a plate and set aside.

In the same sauté pan, melt the butter with the remaining 2 tablespoons olive oil over high heat. Add the livers and quickly sear well on all sides, then sprinkle with salt and pepper. Add the broth, wine, and tomato paste and bring to a boil. Add the reserved mushrooms and the prosciutto, if using, and heat through.

Drain the pasta, add to the sauté pan, and toss and cook with the sauce over low heat for 1 minute. Divide among warmed pasta bowls and serve at once.

# Linguine alle vongole e pomodori

LINGUINE WITH CLAMS

Combining briny steamed clams, dry white wine, tart-sweet tomatoes, earthy herbs, and meaty *sopressata* results in a bright-tasting pasta sauce. The recipe can be doubled but you will need a big pan to accommodate all of the clams. In keeping with the Italian tradition of no cheese on seafood pastas, don't pass Parmesan at the table for this one.  WINE Valpolicella or Barbera  SERVES 4 as a first course or 2 or 3 as a main course

24 MANILA CLAMS (ABOUT 1 ½ POUNDS)

¼ CUP OLIVE OIL

2 CUPS LOOSELY PACKED SLICED RED ONIONS (ABOUT
   ¼ INCH THICK)

3 TO 4 TEASPOONS MINCED GARLIC

GENEROUS PINCH OF RED PEPPER FLAKES

3 OUNCES *SOPRESSATA*, PEELED AND CHOPPED

½ CUP DRY WHITE WINE

1 ⅓ CUPS TOMATO SAUCE, CANNED OR HOMEMADE
   (SEE NOTE, PAGE 140)

1 TEASPOON CHOPPED FRESH ROSEMARY OR 2
   TEASPOONS DRIED OREGANO

SALT

½ POUND LINGUINE OR SPAGHETTI

2 TABLESPOONS CHOPPED FRESH FLAT-LEAF PARSLEY

There are two ways to make this pasta. You can choose to have perfect control and dirty 2 pans, or you can live dangerously and make it in a single pan. (Two pans are an especially good idea if you decide to double the recipe.) Scrub the clams well and keep refrigerated in a bowl of cold water until you need them.

Bring a large pot filled with water to a boil for cooking the pasta.

In a large sauté pan, warm the olive oil over medium heat. Add the onions and cook, stirring occasionally, until softened and golden, about 8 minutes. Add the garlic to taste and the red pepper flakes and continue to cook, stirring occasionally, for 3 minutes longer. Add the *sopressata*, wine, tomato sauce, and rosemary, stir well, and simmer for 3 minutes to blend the flavors. Add the clams, hinge side down, cover the pan, and cook until the clams open, about 5 minutes. Discard any clams that failed to open.

Alternatively, make the sauce as directed, but put the clams and wine in a separate sauté pan or saucepan over medium-heat, cover, and cook until the clams open, about 5 minutes, discarding any that failed to open. Add the clams and their cooking liquid to the sauce.

While the sauce is cooking, add 1 tablespoon salt and then the pasta to the boiling water, stir well, and cook until al dente, according to the package directions.

Drain the pasta, add to the sauté pan, and toss and cook with the sauce over medium heat briefly. Divide among warmed pasta bowls, placing most of the clams on top. Sprinkle with the parsley, dividing it evenly, and serve at once.

# SHOP
# AND
# SERVE
## ANTIPASTI

QUICK BITES

# IN THE OVEN OR ON THE GRILL

DON'T THINK THAT because an oven or grill is used for these suggestions that they are time-consuming or labor-intensive. All of them call for only minimal work and cooking, and the heat heightens the flavors of the salumi.

- Cut figs in half, wrap in prosciutto with a mint leaf, brush lightly with extra virgin olive oil, and broil or grill until the prosciutto is slightly crispy at the edges. Serve hot or warm if possible, or at room temperature.

- Cut figs in half and grill them, brushing them with extra virgin olive oil as they cook. Place the fig halves on prosciutto slices and top the figs with a few drops of aged balsamic vinegar.

- Cut an X in the stem end of each fig and open the fruit like the petals of a tulip. Stuff with a mixture of softened Gorgonzola cheese mixed with chopped walnuts (allow 6 ounces cheese and 2 tablespoons chopped toasted walnuts for 12 figs). Bake in a 450°F oven until warmed through, about 10 minutes. Serve with prosciutto slices.

# Bomba di riso con salumi e formaggi

## BAKED RICE CASSEROLE FILLED WITH SALUMI AND CHEESES

A *bomba* guarantees the cook a dramatic presentation at the table. The filling varies according to what you have on hand. Cooked squab, duck, or chicken, all off of the bone, is fine, as is sausage, mortadella, or meatballs. An assortment of cheeses or cooked vegetables mixed with the cheeses work well, too. This delicious—and simpler— version from Campania adds mortadella, ham, and peas to the cheeses   WINE Nebbiolo, Gattinara, or Barbera   SERVES 8 as a first course or 6 as a main course

5 CUPS WATER

SALT

2 ½ CUPS ARBORIO RICE

4 EGGS, LIGHTLY BEATEN

½ CUP GRATED PARMESAN CHEESE

FRESHLY GROUND BLACK PEPPER

FRESHLY GRATED NUTMEG

1 ½ CUPS (ABOUT ¾ POUND) FRESH WHOLE-MILK
    RICOTTA CHEESE

¾ POUND FRESH MOZZARELLA CHEESE, CUT INTO
    ½-INCH CUBES

3 OUNCES THINLY SLICED PROSCIUTTO, DICED

¾ POUND MORTADELLA, CUT INTO ¼-INCH DICE

1 CUP SHELLED PEAS, COOKED IN BOILING
    WATER JUST UNTIL TENDER AND DRAINED
    (OPTIONAL)

Preheat the oven to 350°F. Butter a 2-quart soufflé dish or other ovenproof casserole.

In a saucepan, bring the water to a boil, salt lightly, and add the rice. Boil until almost tender, about 15 minutes. Drain and transfer to a bowl. Add the eggs and Parmesan to the rice and mix well. Season with salt, pepper, and nutmeg.

In a bowl, combine the ricotta, mozzarella, prosciutto, mortadella, and peas and mix well. Season with salt and pepper.

Pack half of the rice mixture into the prepared dish. Top with the cheese mixture and then with the remaining rice mixture, smoothing the surface. Bake until golden, about 30 minutes. Remove from the oven and let rest for 10 minutes.

Run a knife around the inside of the soufflé dish, invert a platter on top, and, holding the dish and platter together, flip them. Lift off the soufflé dish, slice the *bomba*, and serve at once. To reheat any leftover slices, place in buttered ramekins and reheat in a 350°F oven for 10 minutes.

# Pastuccia

## POLENTA WITH SALUMI AND RAISINS

Two kinds of salumi and golden raisins lace this hearty polenta pie, a specialty of the pre-Roman town of Teramo, in Abruzzo. Be sure to use regular, not instant, polenta or the pie will not cook properly. If serving as a main course, accompany with a salad or green vegetables.   WINE Dolcetto or Montepulciano d'Abruzzo   SERVES 8 to 10 as a first course or 6 as a main course

2 TABLESPOONS OLIVE OIL OR LARD, PLUS MORE
   OLIVE OIL FOR DRIZZLING

¼ POUND PANCETTA, DICED

2 CUPS POLENTA

1 TEASPOON SALT

ABOUT 4 CUPS BOILING WATER

½ POUND *SOPRESSATA*, PEELED AND CHOPPED

1 CUP GOLDEN RAISINS, PLUMPED IN HOT WATER
   AND DRAINED

3 EGG YOLKS

FRESHLY GROUND BLACK PEPPER

Preheat the oven to 375°F. Oil or butter a 12-inch pie dish or a 9-by-12-inch baking dish.

In a large sauté pan, warm the 2 tablespoons olive oil (or melt the lard) over medium heat. Add the pancetta and cook, stirring occasionally, until it renders its fat and is cooked through but not crisp, 5 to 7 minutes. Remove from the heat.

In a large bowl, combine the polenta and salt. Gradually whisk in enough boiling water to make a very thick batter. Add three-fourths each of the pancetta and *sopressata*, the raisins, the egg yolks, and some pepper and mix well. Pour into the prepared dish. Top evenly with the remaining pancetta and *sopressata* and drizzle with a little olive oil.

Bake until the top is golden and the pancetta is crisp, about 40 minutes. Let cool for about 10 minutes before serving.

# Secondi

## MAIN COURSES

MANY TYPICAL ITALIAN *secondi piatti*, or main courses, are relatively simple dishes, such as panfried trout (page 104), sautéed shrimp (page 107), or veal scaloppine (page 113). Others, such as a stuffed rolled veal leg (page 114) or a slow-cooked beef stew (page 121), take a little more work and time. Both of these traditions appear in this chapter. But all of the *secondi* here share a reliance on the rich, sophisticated flavor of salumi for their success, sometimes used as a wrap, other times as a flavoring in a stuffing or sauce, and still others as the centerpiece, as in Cotechino and Lentils (page 103). ◈

# Calamari ripieni

## STUFFED SQUID

Squid are a natural vehicle for stuffing, especially with a mixture that includes salumi, and now that you can buy them already cleaned at your market, they do not seem so daunting to prepare. Keep in mind that for squid to be tender, you must cook them for just a few minutes or allow them to braise for an hour. There is no middle ground.   WINE Arneis or Pinot Grigio   SERVES 4

12 MEDIUM-SIZED SQUID, CLEANED WITH BODIES
    AND TENTACLES LEFT WHOLE (ABOUT 1 ½ POUNDS
    AFTER CLEANING)

¼ POUND MORTADELLA, PEELED AND FINELY CHOPPED

½ CUP DRIED PORCINI MUSHROOMS, SOAKED IN
    HOT WATER TO COVER FOR 30 MINUTES, DRAINED,
    AND CHOPPED

¼ CUP CHOPPED FRESH FLAT-LEAF PARSLEY

2 CLOVES GARLIC, MINCED

¾ CUP GRATED PARMESAN CHEESE

3 EGGS, LIGHTLY BEATEN

1 ITALIAN BREAD ROLL OR 2 THICK SLICES COARSE
    COUNTRY BREAD, CRUSTS REMOVED, SOAKED IN
    MILK, AND SQUEEZED ALMOST DRY

SALT AND FRESHLY GROUND BLACK PEPPER

¼ CUP EXTRA VIRGIN OLIVE OIL, PLUS MORE
    FOR FINISHING

1 YELLOW ONION, CHOPPED

1 CELERY STALK, CHOPPED

ABOUT 1 ½ CUPS DRY WHITE WINE

LEMON WEDGES FOR SERVING

Rinse the squid bodies and tentacles well under running cold water, drain well, and reserve the bodies and tentacles separately.

To make the stuffing, in a bowl, combine the mortadella, porcini, parsley, and garlic and mix well. Add the cheese, eggs, and bread and mix well. Season with salt and pepper. Or, combine the ingredients in the same order in a food processor and pulse to mix. (Large pieces in the stuffing can dam up the pastry bag, and the processor helps avoid that.) Using a pastry bag fitted with a large plain tip or a small spoon, fill the squid bodies with the stuffing, and skewer closed with toothpicks.

In a sauté pan large enough to hold all of the squid in a single layer, warm the ¼ cup olive oil over medium heat. Add the onion and celery and cook, stirring occasionally, until softened, about 8 minutes. Add the tentacles and cook, stirring, for 2 minutes longer. Add the stuffed squid and pour in the wine to reach halfway up the sides of the squid. Season with salt and pepper, cover, reduce the heat to low, and cook until the squid are tender, 40 to 60 minutes. Check the liquid level a few times and add more wine if needed to maintain the same level. Remove from the heat.

Transfer the squid and pan juices to a shallow platter and drizzle with olive oil. Serve warm or at room temperature with lemon wedges.

# Cotechino e lenticchie

## COTECHINO AND LENTILS

You can use either *cotechino* or *zampone*, both specialties of the Emilia-Romagna city of Modena, for this dish. The latter is a pig's trotter stuffed with a sausage mixture, while *cotechino* is the same sausage mixture but in a traditional casing. *Zampone* requires overnight soaking and then about 4 hours of cooking. Precooked versions are available that eliminate the soaking step and cook in about 45 minutes. Choosing between the trotter and the sausage for this dish comes down to whether you like the thick, rather gelatinous rind—the skin of the trotter—that covers the *zampone*.   WINE Barbera   SERVES 8

2 CUPS ITALIAN OR FRENCH GREEN LENTILS,
   RINSED AND DRAINED

SALT

ABOUT ½ CUP OLIVE OIL

¼ POUND PANCETTA, DICED

1 ½ CUPS CHOPPED YELLOW ONIONS

½ CUP PEELED, DICED CARROTS

½ CUP DICED CELERY

1 TABLESPOON MINCED GARLIC

1 CUP PEELED, SEEDED, AND CHOPPED FRESH
   TOMATOES OR CANNED PLUM TOMATOES

FRESHLY GROUND BLACK PEPPER

1 *COTECHINO*, 2 TO 3 POUNDS

2 OR 3 BAY LEAVES

In a saucepan, combine the lentils with water to cover by 2 inches. Bring to a boil over medium-high heat, reduce the heat to low, add 2 teaspoons salt, and simmer gently, uncovered, until tender but not falling apart, 30 to 40 minutes.

While the lentils are cooking, in a sauté pan, warm ¼ cup of the olive oil over medium heat. Add the pancetta, onions, carrots, and celery and cook, stirring occasionally, until the vegetables are tender, 10 to 15 minutes. Add the garlic and tomatoes and cook for a few minutes longer.

When the lentils are ready, remove from the heat, drain, add to the tomato mixture, and toss to combine. Taste and adjust the seasoning with salt and pepper. Remove from the heat and then reheat just before serving.

To cook the *cotechino*, place it in a saucepan with lightly salted water to cover. Toss in the bay leaves and bring to a boil over medium-high heat. Reduce the heat to low and simmer, uncovered, until the sausage is cooked through, 45 to 60 minutes.

Remove the *cotechino* from the pan, drain well, place on a cutting board, and pat dry. Cut into ½-inch-thick slices and arrange on a warmed platter. Serve at once with the lentils.

# Trota con prosciutto

## TROUT WRAPPED WITH PROSCIUTTO

There are two ways to cook this simple dish. You can cook the fish and mushrooms separately, deglaze the pan used for the fish with a little wine, reheat the mushrooms in the pan juices, and spoon them alongside the fish. Or, you can grill the fish and serve them with sautéed mushrooms. Both ways are included here. Roasted or boiled potatoes and sautéed spinach are excellent accompaniments.   **WINE** Rosato, Pinot Noir, or Tocai Friulano   **SERVES** 4

4 FRESHWATER TROUT, CLEANED WITH HEADS ON, EACH ABOUT 3/4 POUND

SALT AND FRESHLY GROUND BLACK PEPPER

8 THIN SLICES PROSCIUTTO

8 FRESH SAGE LEAVES

3 TABLESPOONS UNSALTED BUTTER

1 1/2 CUPS SLICED FRESH MUSHROOMS SUCH AS WHITE OR CREMINI

ALL-PURPOSE FLOUR OR EQUAL PARTS ALL-PURPOSE FLOUR AND CORNMEAL FOR DUSTING

1/3 CUP OLIVE OIL

1/4 CUP DRY WHITE WINE

LEMON WEDGES FOR SERVING

Sprinkle the trout inside and out with salt and pepper. Stuff 1 slice of prosciutto and 2 sage leaves inside each trout cavity, and then wrap 1 slice of prosciutto around each trout. (You don't need to skewer the fish closed with toothpicks or tie them with string because the prosciutto wrap holds the stuffing in and a light dusting with flour keeps the wrap in place.)

In a small sauté pan, melt the butter over medium heat. Add the mushrooms and cook, stirring occasionally, just until they wilt, 3 to 5 minutes. Transfer to a plate and set aside.

Spread some flour on a large plate. In a large sauté pan, warm the olive oil over medium-high heat. When the oil is hot, one at a time, dip the trout in the flour, coating evenly and tapping off the excess, and add to the pan. Fry, turning once, until golden on both sides and the flesh is just opaque when tested with the tip of a knife, 3 to 4 minutes on each side. Transfer the trout to warmed individual plates and keep warm.

Pour the wine into the pan over medium-high heat. Bring to a simmer and deglaze the pan, dislodging any browned bits stuck to the pan bottom. Add the reserved mushrooms and warm through.

Spoon the mushrooms over or alongside the trout. Serve at once with lemon wedges.

*Grilled Variation:* Prepare a medium-hot fire in a grill. Prepare the fish as directed but do not dust with flour. Brush the wrapped fish with olive oil. Grill the trout directly over the fire, turning once, until golden on both sides and the flesh is just opaque when tested with the tip of a knife, 3 to 4 minutes on each side. Serve with mushrooms sautéed in butter and with lemon wedges, or with only lemon wedges.

# Gamberi o capesante con pancetta

## SHRIMP OR SCALLOPS WRAPPED WITH PANCETTA

The saltiness of pancetta delivers a wonderful contrast to the sweetness of the shellfish in this quick and easy dish. As is the case with the trout on page 104, the shrimp or scallops can also be grilled instead of sautéed (see variation). Serve atop a bed of salad greens, wilted spinach, or cooked white beans or lentils.   WINE Fiano d'Avellino, Falanghina, or Vermentino   SERVES 4

6 TO 8 PAPER-THIN SLICES PANCETTA (NOT TOO LEAN)
12 JUMBO OR 16 LARGE SHRIMP, PEELED AND DEVEINED,
    OR 12 LARGE SEA SCALLOPS, FOOT MUSCLE REMOVED
FRESHLY GROUND BLACK PEPPER
¼ CUP EXTRA VIRGIN OLIVE OIL
¼ CUP COGNAC
LEMON WEDGES FOR SERVING

Cut each pancetta slice—6 slices if using jumbo shrimp or scallops and 8 slices if using large shrimp—in half crosswise so you have a total of 12 or 16 pieces. Wrap each shrimp or scallop in a half slice of pancetta. Sprinkle with pepper.

In a large sauté pan, warm the olive oil over medium-high heat. Add the shrimp or scallops and sauté quickly, turning once, until the shrimp turn pink, or the scallops firm up a bit and take on some color, and the pancetta becomes golden, 4 to 6 minutes. Transfer to warmed individual plates.

Pour the Cognac into the pan over medium-high heat. Bring to a simmer and deglaze the pan, dislodging any browned bits stuck to the pan bottom.

Spoon the pan juices over the shellfish. Serve at once with lemon wedges.

*Grilled or Broiled Variation:* Prepare a medium-hot fire in a grill or preheat a broiler. Soak 4 bamboo skewers in water to cover for about 30 minutes, then drain. Wrap the shrimp or scallops with pancetta as directed and thread onto the skewers. Brush with olive oil and sprinkle with pepper. Grill the seafood directly over the fire, or under the preheated broiler, turning once, until the shrimp turn pink, or the scallops firm up a bit and take on some color, and the pancetta becomes golden, 3 to 4 minutes on each side. Serve with lemon wedges.

# Petti di pollo ripieni

## STUFFED CHICKEN BREASTS

Cooks are always looking for ways to infuse the white meat of chicken with flavor. Stuffing the breasts with a savory filling is one tasty solution. These rolled chicken breasts are tender and juicy and may be served hot or at room temperature. They also make a nice antipasto for eight.  WINE Chianti Classico or Barbera  SERVES 4

2 TABLESPOONS OLIVE OIL, PLUS MORE FOR BRUSHING

1 SMALL YELLOW ONION, FINELY CHOPPED

2 CLOVES GARLIC, MINCED

1 CUP FINELY CHOPPED MORTADELLA

½ CUP MIXED CHOPPED FRESH HERBS SUCH AS FLAT-LEAF PARSLEY, BASIL, SAGE, AND/OR ROSEMARY, IN ANY COMBINATION

4 CUPS FRESH BREAD CRUMBS, LIGHTLY TOASTED

4 EGGS, LIGHTLY BEATEN

SALT AND FRESHLY GROUND BLACK PEPPER

8 SKINLESS, BONELESS CHICKEN BREAST HALVES, ABOUT 6 OUNCES EACH

1 LEMON, HALVED (OPTIONAL)

1 ½ CUPS TOMATO SAUCE, CANNED OR HOMEMADE (SEE NOTE, PAGE 140), WARMED (OPTIONAL)

MAYONNAISE SEASONED TO TASTE WITH MUSTARD FOR SERVING (OPTIONAL)

To make the stuffing, in a small sauté pan, warm the 2 tablespoons olive oil. Add the onion and cook, stirring occasionally, until softened, 5 to 7 minutes. Add the garlic and cook for a minute or two to soften its bite. Transfer to a bowl. Add the mortadella, herbs, bread crumbs, and eggs and mix well. Season with salt and pepper and mix again.

Preheat the oven to 375°F. Oil a baking dish that will accommodate the stuffed breasts in a single layer.

Place each chicken breast half between 2 sheets of plastic wrap and, using a meat pounder, pound until thin, making sure the breast is of uniform thickness. Sprinkle each breast with salt and pepper. Place an equal amount of stuffing near one end of each breast. Fold over the end, tuck in the sides, and roll up. Tie the roll securely with kitchen string. Brush the rolled breasts with olive oil, and sprinkle with salt and pepper.

Arrange the rolled breasts in the prepared dish and cover with aluminum foil. Bake until firm to the touch and opaque throughout when tested with a knife tip, 15 to 20 minutes.

Remove from the oven and transfer the rolls to a cutting board. Snip the strings and cut the rolls crosswise into slices about ½ inch thick. Arrange the slices on a warmed serving platter or individual plates, and squeeze lemon juice over the tops. Or, spoon the tomato sauce onto the platter or plates and arrange the slices on top.

Alternatively, remove from the oven, let cool, cover, and refrigerate until cold. Snip the strings and cut the rolls crosswise into slices ½ inch thick. Serve at room temperature with mustard mayonnaise.

# QUICK
# MAIN
# COURSES

### THREE SIMPLE DISHES

# EASY SALUMI MEALS

**SALAME NEL ACETO  SALAME WITH VINEGAR**

For this dish from Friuli, cut 1-inch-thick slices from a young salame and sauté in olive oil or lard over medium heat until lightly colored on both sides. Transfer to a plate. Add red wine vinegar to the pan, about 3 tablespoons per slice, and deglaze the pan over medium-high heat, stirring to dislodge any browned bits on the pan bottom and cooking until the vinegar is syrupy. Arrange the sautéed salame over slices of grilled or fried polenta and spoon the pan juices on top. Pour a regional Merlot or Cabernet Sauvignon.

**COPPA AL MARSALA  COPPA WITH MARSALA**

For this dish from Emilia-Romagna, rub thick slices of young *coppa* with fresh herbs, arrange the slices in a single layer in a baking dish, and place in a 350°F oven. Bake, basting frequently with dry Marsala, until the *coppa* is soft and tender. Cut into strips or segments and serve with mashed potatoes. Pour a regional Sangiovese.

**SALAME E PATATE  SALAME WITH POTATOES**

For this dish from Carnia in Friuli, peel 1 1/2 pounds boiling or baking potatoes and cut into small cubes. Peel a small salame, like *crespone* or *salametto*, and slice thinly to yield about 1/4 pound. In a sauté pan, warm 1/4 cup olive oil over medium heat. Add the salame slices and sauté until golden, 4 to 5 minutes. Remove with a slotted spoon and set aside. Add the potatoes to the fat in the pan, stir well, and then brown on all sides, turning as needed. Add 1 cup boiling water, top with the reserved salame slices, cover, and cook over low heat until the potatoes are tender and perfumed with the salame, about 15 minutes. Season to taste with freshly ground black pepper and serve at once. Pour a Refosco or Merlot.

# Saltimbocca alla romana

## VEAL SCALOPPINE WITH PROSCIUTTO AND SAGE

This Roman classic takes its name from *saltare*, which means "to jump," and *bocca*, which means "mouth." Not an understatement for such a delicious dish. The veal should be cut from the leg and pounded gently. Deglazing the pan with a little broth and wine makes a light, tasty sauce. Serve with mashed potatoes and spinach or broccoli.   WINE Nebbiolo d'Alba, Chianti, Barbera, or Frascati   **SERVES** 4

8 SLICES VEAL, EACH ⅓ INCH THICK (ABOUT 1
  POUND TOTAL)

16 FRESH SAGE LEAVES

8 SLICES PROSCIUTTO

ALL-PURPOSE FLOUR FOR DUSTING

SALT AND FRESHLY GROUND BLACK PEPPER

4 TABLESPOONS UNSALTED BUTTER

2 TABLESPOONS OLIVE OIL

½ CUP MEAT BROTH

¼ CUP DRY MARSALA OR DRY WHITE WINE

One at a time, place each veal slice between 2 sheets of plastic wrap and, using a meat pounder, pound gently to a uniform thickness of about ¼ inch.

Lay 2 sage leaves on each veal slice, and then top with a slice of prosciutto. Secure the prosciutto in place with toothpicks. Spread some flour on a large plate and season with salt and pepper.

In a large sauté pan, melt 2 tablespoons of the butter with the olive oil over medium heat. Working in batches to avoid crowding, lightly dust the veal bundles evenly with the flour, tapping off the excess, and place in the pan, prosciutto side down. Sauté until golden on the first side, about 4 minutes. Turn and cook on the second side, about 3 minutes longer. Transfer to a warmed platter and keep warm. Repeat with the remaining veal bundles.

Discard the excess fat from the pan, return the pan to high heat, and add the broth and wine. Deglaze the pan, stirring to dislodge the browned bits on the pan bottom and reducing the liquid by half. Swirl in the remaining 2 tablespoons butter.

Pour the pan sauce evenly over the veal and serve at once.

*Variation with Chicken:* Substitute 8 boneless, skinless chicken breast halves for the veal slices and proceed as directed.

# Rollata di vitello alla piemontese

## BRAISED STUFFED LEG OF VEAL FROM THE PIEDMONT

This delicately flavored *rollata*, a specialty of Piedmont, makes a particularly elegant main course.  **WINE** Dolcetto d'Alba, Barbera, or Nebbiolo d'Alba  **SERVES** 6

1 BONELESS LEG OF VEAL, 3 TO 4 POUNDS

2 CLOVES GARLIC, FINELY CHOPPED

1 TABLESPOON FRESH ROSEMARY LEAVES, FINELY
    CHOPPED, PLUS 2 SPRIGS

SALT AND FRESHLY GROUND BLACK PEPPER

FRESHLY GRATED NUTMEG

6 THIN SLICES PROSCIUTTO (NOT PAPER-THIN)

6 THIN SLICES MORTADELLA

6 TABLESPOONS UNSALTED BUTTER

1 TABLESPOON OLIVE OIL

2 YELLOW ONIONS, CUT INTO ¼-INCH DICE (ABOUT
    3 CUPS)

3 SMALL CARROTS, PEELED AND CUT INTO ¼-INCH DICE
    (ABOUT 1 CUP)

3 CELERY STALKS, CUT INTO ¼-INCH DICE (ABOUT 1 CUP)

1 ½ TO 2 CUPS DRY WHITE WINE

1 ½ TO 2 CUPS CHICKEN OR VEAL BROTH

To butterfly the leg, place it on a clean, scratch-proof work surface and, using a long, sharp knife, cut it nearly in half horizontally, stopping within about ½ inch of the opposite side. Lay it flat, like a book, and trim away any visible gristle and tendons and any excess fat. Place the meat between 2 sheets of plastic wrap and, using a meat pounder, pound it to a uniform thickness of about 1 inch.

In a bowl, stir together the garlic, chopped rosemary, and a little salt and pepper. Spread the mixture evenly over the meat. Grate a light dusting of nutmeg over the garlic mixture, then lay the slices of prosciutto and mortadella on top. Roll up the veal, and tie with kitchen string at

1-inch intervals. Slip the 2 rosemary sprigs under the string binding the roll. Sprinkle the veal evenly with salt and pepper, then season lightly with nutmeg.

In a large Dutch oven, melt 3 tablespoons of the butter with the olive oil over medium-high heat. Add the veal and brown on all sides, 10 to 15 minutes. Use 2 wooden spoons or tongs, transfer to a plate and set aside.

Add the onions, carrots, and celery to the fat remaining in the pan over medium heat and cook, stirring occasionally, until softened and pale gold, about 12 minutes. Return the veal to the pan and add the wine and broth, in equal amounts, almost to cover the roast. Gradually bring to a boil over medium heat. Reduce the heat to low, cover, and simmer until tender when pierced with a knife or an instant-read meat thermometer inserted into the thickest part of the roll registers 140°F, about 1 ½ hours.

Transfer the veal to a carving board, cover with aluminum foil to keep warm, and let rest for about 15 minutes before cutting. Meanwhile, reduce the pan juices over high heat until you have about 1 ½ cups, then whisk in the remaining 3 tablespoons butter to thicken.

Snip the strings on the meat and cut crosswise into slices about ¼ inch thick. Arrange the slices on a warmed platter and spoon the pan juices and braising vegetables over the top. Serve at once.

# Favata

## SARDINIAN PORK AND BEAN STEW

Spain's influence on the Sardinian table is evident in this savory bean and sausage stew that resembles a classic Asturian *fabada*. **WINE** Torgiano Rosso or Cannonau   **SERVES** 4 to 6

### BEANS

2 CUPS (ABOUT 14 OUNCES) DRIED WHITE BEANS OR
    FAVA BEANS, SOAKED OVERNIGHT IN WATER TO
    COVER, DRAINED, AND RINSED

1 YELLOW ONION, CHOPPED

2 CLOVES GARLIC, PEELED BUT LEFT WHOLE

1 BAY LEAF

SALT AND FRESHLY GROUND BLACK PEPPER

4 SWEET FENNEL SAUSAGES (ABOUT 1 POUND TOTAL)
    OR 1 POUND *COTECHINO*

OLIVE OIL

¼ POUND PANCETTA, CHOPPED

1 YELLOW ONION, CHOPPED

3 CLOVES GARLIC, MINCED

2 OR 3 TOMATOES, PEELED, SEEDED, AND CHOPPED

½ CUP MEAT BROTH OR WATER

½ CUP DRY WHITE WINE

2 TO 3 TABLESPOONS CHOPPED FRESH MINT

SALT AND FRESHLY GROUND BLACK PEPPER

GRATED PECORINO CHEESE FOR SERVING

To cook the beans, in a saucepan, combine the soaked beans, onion, garlic, and bay leaf with water to cover by about 1 ½ inches and bring to a boil over medium-high heat. Reduce the heat to low and simmer, uncovered, until the beans are tender, 40 to 60 minutes. Remove from the heat and season with salt and pepper. Discard the bay leaf and set the beans aside in their liquid.

If using fennel sausages, prick each sausage with a fork in a few places, place in a skillet, and add water to the pan to a depth of about ½ inch. Place over medium heat and cook, uncovered, until the sausages are cooked through, about 10 minutes. Remove from the heat, let the sausages cool slightly until they can be handled, and then cut into chunks and set aside. If using *cotechino*, peel away the casing, cut the sausage into thick slices, place in a skillet, and add water just to cover. Place over medium heat and cook, uncovered, until the slices are firm, 10 to 15 minutes. Remove from the heat, drain off the water, and set aside.

Place a large saucepan over medium-high heat and film the bottom with olive oil. Add the pancetta and fry until it renders its fat and is crispy, about 8 minutes. Using a slotted spoon, transfer to a plate and set aside.

Add the onion to the fat remaining in the pan over medium heat and cook, stirring occasionally, until the onion is softened and translucent, about 8 minutes. Add the garlic and tomatoes and cook for 3 minutes longer. Add the broth, wine, reserved sausages and pancetta, and mint to the pan and simmer for 10 minutes.

Drain the beans, reserving the liquid, and add the beans to the sausage mixture. Bring to a simmer, adding some of the bean liquid if the liquid in the pan has reduced too much. Cover, reduce the heat to low, and simmer for 10 minutes to blend the flavors.

Season the stew to taste with salt and pepper and serve at once. Pass the pecorino at the table.

# Spezzatino di maiale alla triestina

## PORK STEW WITH FENNEL FRONDS AND TOMATO FROM TRIESTE

Unless you grow your own fennel, or shop at a farmers' market, fennel greens may be hard to find. At most markets, the produce clerks trim the feathery fronds off the bulbs and throw them away. However, seeking them out is worth the effort for the subtle anise note they add to this stew. Cumin is a signature flavor in the kitchens of Trieste, and toasting the seeds before crushing them brings out their distinctive flavor. This stew is often served with *polenta saracena*, a mixture of polenta and buckwheat, but plain polenta or mashed potatoes would be good as well. WINE Refosco or Merlot from Friuli SERVES 4 or 5

2 TABLESPOONS CHOPPED PANCETTA FAT OR LARD

1/4 POUND PANCETTA, CHOPPED

2 POUNDS BONELESS PORK SHOULDER, CUT INTO 1- TO 1 1/2-INCH CUBES

SALT AND FRESHLY GROUND BLACK PEPPER

1 YELLOW ONION, CHOPPED

1 TABLESPOON CUMIN SEEDS, TOASTED IN A DRY PAN OVER LOW HEAT UNTIL FRAGRANT AND THEN COARSELY GROUND IN A SPICE MILL

2 TABLESPOONS MINCED GARLIC

2 CUPS CHOPPED FENNEL FRONDS

1 1/2 CUPS PEELED, SEEDED, AND CHOPPED FRESH TOMATOES OR CANNED PLUM TOMATOES

1/2 CUP MEAT BROTH OR WATER, OR AS NEEDED

In a Dutch oven or large sauté pan, render the fat or melt the lard over high heat. Add the pancetta and fry, stirring often, until golden, 5 to 7 minutes. Using a slotted spoon, transfer to a plate and set aside.

Working in batches to avoid crowding, add the pork cubes to the fat remaining in the pan over medium-high heat and brown well on all sides, seasoning with salt and pepper as you turn the meat. Each batch should take 8 to 10 minutes. As each batch is ready, use the slotted spoon to transfer the meat to a plate. Set aside.

Add the onion, cumin, and garlic to the fat remaining in the pan over medium heat and cook, stirring occasionally, until the onion has softened, about 5 minutes. Return the pancetta and pork to the pan and add the fennel fronds, tomatoes, and 1/2 cup broth. Bring to a gentle boil, reduce the heat to low, cover, and simmer until the pork is tender, about 1 1/2 hours. Check from time to time and add more broth if needed to prevent sticking.

Season the stew to taste with salt and pepper. Serve at once.

# SHOP
# AND
# SERVE
## ANTIPASTI

HIDDEN FLAVORS

# ROLL UPS

ONE OF THE EASIEST WAYS to dress up your antipasto presentation is to conceal a tasty surprise inside a slice of salumi.

- Roll slices of salame around dollops of herbed goat cheese or cream cheese. Spear with toothpicks, if desired.

- Spread mortadella slices with Dijon mustard mixed with enough mayonnaise to mellow the bite of the mustard. Top with strips of provolone cheese, roll up, and spear with toothpicks.

- Combine 7 ounces Gorgonzola *dolcelatte* cheese and ¼ pound mascarpone cheese and mash together until well mixed. Add 3 tablespoons finely chopped toasted walnuts and 2 tablespoons finely chopped fresh flat-leaf parsley and mix well. Spread the cheese mixture on mortadella slices (about 6 ounces) and roll up. Cut the rolls into bite-sized pieces, if desired, and spear with toothpicks.

# Spiedini di maiale alla campagna

PORK BROCHETTES WITH PROSCIUTTO AND LEMON-SAGE BUTTER

The prosciutto wrap in this dish adds just the right amount of sweetness and saltiness, and a dab of lemon-sage butter completes the flavor profile.   WINE Barbaresco or *Taurasi*   SERVES 8

### MARINADE

1 CUP OLIVE OIL

4 FRESH SAGE LEAVES, COARSELY CHOPPED

2 CLOVES GARLIC, CRUSHED

3 TABLESPOONS FRESH LEMON JUICE

3 OR 4 LEMON ZEST STRIPS

2 ½ POUNDS PORK TENDERLOIN, TRIMMED OF
   SILVER SKIN AND CUT INTO 1 ½-INCH CUBES (16 TO
   18 CUBES TOTAL)

16 TO 18 FRESH SAGE LEAVES

8 OR 9 THIN SLICES PROSCIUTTO, CUT IN HALF
   LENGTHWISE

SALT AND FRESHLY GROUND BLACK PEPPER

### LEMON-SAGE BUTTER

¾ CUP UNSALTED BUTTER, AT ROOM TEMPERATURE

2 TABLESPOONS FRESH LEMON JUICE

GRATE ZEST OF 1 TO 2 LEMONS

2 TABLESPOONS CHOPPED FRESH SAGE, OR AS NEEDED

SALT AND FRESHLY GROUND BLACK PEPPER

To make the marinade, in a small saucepan, warm the olive oil over medium heat until hot to the touch. Remove from the heat and add the sage, garlic, lemon juice, and lemon zest. Let stand until completely cooled, about 1 hour.

Place the pork in a baking dish or shallow bowl, pour the marinade over the top, and turn the cubes to coat evenly. The marinade should just cover the meat. Cover and marinate in the refrigerator overnight. If you remember, turn the meat occasionally, though this is not crucial if the marinade covers the meat well.

The next day, soak about 6 wooden bamboo skewers in water to cover for about 30 minutes. Prepare a medium-hot fire in a grill or preheat the broiler.

To assemble the brochettes, drain the meat, reserving the marinade. Drain the skewers. Place a sage leaf on each piece of meat and wrap them together in a piece of prosciutto. Thread 3 meat cubes onto each skewer.

To make the lemon-sage butter, in a food processor, combine the butter, lemon juice, half of the lemon zest, and 2 tablespoons sage and process until smooth. Season to taste with salt and pepper, then taste and add more lemon zest and/or sage as needed. Set the butter aside at room temperature so it remains soft enough to spread.

Season the brochettes with salt and pepper and brush with some of the marinade. Grill directly over the fire, or under the broiler, until nicely browned, about 5 minutes. Turn, brush with a little more marinade, and cook until nicely browned on the second side and the meat tests done when pierced with a knife, about 5 minutes longer.

Remove the pork cubes from the skewers and spread each one generously with the lemon-sage butter. Serve at once.

# Stufatino di manzo peposo

TUSCAN PEPPERY BEEF STEW

Known affectionately as *il peposo*, "the peppery one," this tongue-tingling beef ragout is a Tuscan specialty, attributed to both the hill town of Impruneta and to the town of Versilia.    WINE Chianti Classico or Morellino di Scansano    SERVES 6

MARINADE

3 TO 4 TABLESPOONS OLIVE OIL

½ CUP DRY RED WINE

1 TABLESPOON FRESHLY GROUND BLACK PEPPER

SALT

3 POUNDS BONELESS STEWING BEEF SUCH AS CHUCK
    OR BRISKET, CUT INTO 2-INCH PIECES

1 CAN (28 OUNCES) PLUM TOMATOES, WITH JUICES

3 TO 4 TABLESPOONS OLIVE OIL

2 CUPS DRY RED WINE

½ POUND PANCETTA, CUT INTO ¼-INCH DICE

3 LARGE YELLOW ONIONS, CHOPPED

6 CLOVES GARLIC, FINELY MINCED

FRESHLY GROUND BLACK PEPPER

1 CUP BEEF BROTH

To make the marinade, in a baking dish or shallow bowl, stir together the olive oil, wine, pepper, and a little salt.

Add the meat, turn to coat, cover, and marinate overnight in the refrigerator. Drain the meat, pat dry, and bring the meat to room temperature (about 30 minutes) before cooking.

Place the tomatoes and their juices in a food processor and process until finely chopped but not liquefied. Set aside.

In a heavy sauté pan, warm the olive oil over high heat. Working in batches, add the beef pieces and brown well on all sides. Each batch should take about 10 minutes.

As each batch is ready, use a slotted spoon to transfer the meat to a Dutch oven or other large, heavy pan. Then add 1 cup of the wine to the sauté pan, bring to a boil, and deglaze the pan, stirring to dislodge the browned bits from the pan bottom. Pour the pan juices into the Dutch oven.

Return the sauté pan to medium heat, add the pancetta, and cook, stirring occasionally, until it renders some of its fat, 3 to 5 minutes. Add the onions and cook, stirring occasionally, until the onions are softened and translucent and the pancetta is tender but not crisp, about 8 minutes longer. Add the garlic and 2 tablespoons pepper, mix well, and cook for a minute or two to blend the flavors.

Add the onion mixture, the remaining 1 cup wine, the reserved tomatoes, and the broth to the beef in the Dutch oven, place over medium heat, and bring to a gentle boil. Reduce the heat to low, cover, and simmer until the meat is tender, 2 to 2 ½ hours.

Uncover and check the viscosity of the sauce. If necessary, raise the heat to reduce the stewing liquid until it is thick and rich. Taste at this point to see if any salt is needed (the pancetta may have imparted enough salt to the stew) and adjust the pepper to suit your palate. The taste should be quite robust and peppery. Serve at once.

# Braciola alla siciliana

## SICILIAN STUFFED MEAT ROLL

Unlike the small pork rolls called *braciolettine*, braciola is a medium-sized meat roll (and a *braciolone* is a big roll). In this recipe, it is stuffed with slices of mortadella or prosciutto and braised.   **WINE** Nero d'Avola, Barolo, Primitivo, or Aglianico   **SERVES** 6

2 1/2 POUNDS ROUND STEAK, IN A SINGLE PIECE

1/2 POUND GROUND BEEF

2 SLICES COARSE COUNTRY BREAD, CRUSTS REMOVED,
    SOAKED IN WATER, AND SQUEEZED DRY

1 RAW EGG, LIGHTLY BEATEN

3 TABLESPOONS CHOPPED FRESH FLAT-LEAF PARSLEY

SALT AND FRESHLY GROUND BLACK PEPPER

4 THIN SLICES MORTADELLA

4 THIN SLICES PROSCIUTTO

4 HARD-BOILED EGGS, PEELED

1/4 POUND *CACIOCAVALLO* OR PROVOLONE CHEESE,
    CUT INTO STRIPS 1/2 INCH WIDE AND THICK AND
    3 INCHES LONG

OLIVE OIL AS NEEDED

3 CUPS CHOPPED YELLOW ONIONS

4 CUPS TOMATO PUREE

2 CUPS DRY RED WINE

To butterfly the steak, place it on a clean, scratch-proof work surface and, using a long, sharp knife, cut it nearly in half horizontally, stopping within about 1/2 inch of the opposite side. Lay it flat, like a book, and trim away any visible gristle and tendons and any excess fat. Place the meat between 2 sheets of plastic wrap and, using a meat pounder, pound it to a uniform thickness of about 1/2 inch.

In a bowl, combine the ground beef, bread, raw egg, parsley, and a little salt and pepper and mix well.

Place the pounded steak, cut side up, on a clean work surface. Spread the ground meat mixture evenly over the steak. Lay the mortadella slices and then the prosciutto slices evenly on top. Arrange the hard-boiled eggs in a row down the center of the filling. Lay the cheese strips along both sides of the eggs, distributing them evenly. Working from a long side, roll up the beef, and then tie at regular intervals with kitchen string along the length of the roll to secure in place.

Place a sauté pan large enough to accommodate the meat roll over high heat and film the bottom with olive oil. Add the meat roll and brown well on all sides, 10 to 15 minutes. Transfer to a plate and set aside.

In a Dutch oven or other large, heavy pan, heat 3 tablespoons olive oil over medium heat. Add the onions and cook, stirring occasionally, until softened, about 8 minutes. Add the tomato puree and wine and bring to a boil. Add the meat roll, cover, reduce the heat to low, and simmer gently until the meat is tender when tested with a knife tip, about 2 hours.

Transfer the meat roll to a cutting board and let rest for about 10 minutes. Snip the strings and cut the roll crosswise into slices about 1/2 inch thick. Arrange the slices on a warmed platter. Reheat the pan sauce and season with salt and pepper. Spoon some of the sauce over the slices and serve at once.

# Insalate e Contorni

## SALADS AND VEGETABLES

SOME SALADS IN THE Italian repertoire, such as Salad of Oranges, Onions, and Coppa (page 131) or Salad of Figs, Prosciutto, Gorgonzola, and Hazelnuts (page 128), often turn up as an antipasto, while others, usually just a simple mixture of greens or sometimes greens with a little shredded carrot and a few tomato wedges, typically accompany the main course. The latter appear on a menu under the heading *contorni*, or vegetable side dishes, along with such preparations as Peas with Prosciutto (page 133). The addition of salumi to all of the salad and vegetable recipes in this chapter adds an important layer of flavor to the dishes. It also makes many of them substantial enough to serve as the centerpiece of a light lunch or supper.

# Insalata capricciosa

## SALAD WITH CUCUMBERS, CARROTS, CHICKPEAS, AND SALAME

*Capricciosa* means on a whim or as the spirit moves you. The base of the salad can be torn leaves of romaine lettuce, as it is here, or it can be butter or red leaf lettuce or even a mixture of mild lettuces. Then, in moderation, you can add whatever you like, from fennel, mushrooms, mortadella, and mozzarella to the cucumber, carrot, chickpeas, salame, and pecorino used here.  **SERVES** 6

**GARLIC VINAIGRETTE**

¼ CUP EXTRA VIRGIN OLIVE OIL

¼ CUP PURE OLIVE OIL

3 TABLESPOONS RED WINE VINEGAR

1 TEASPOON FINELY MINCED GARLIC

SALT AND FRESHLY GROUND BLACK PEPPER

1 ½ CUPS WELL-DRAINED COOKED CHICKPEAS, HOME
    COOKED OR CANNED

12 CUPS TORN ROMAINE LETTUCE

2 CUPS PEELED, SEEDED, AND DICED CUCUMBERS

1 CUP PEELED, GRATED CARROTS

12 THIN SLICES SALAME, CUT INTO NARROW STRIPS

SMALL WEDGE OF PECORINO OR *RICOTTA
    SALATA* CHEESE

To make the vinaigrette, in a small bowl, whisk together both olive oils, the vinegar, and the garlic. Whisk in salt and pepper to taste.

If using canned chickpeas, rinse and drain well. In a small bowl, combine the chickpeas with ¼ cup of the vinaigrette, stir to coat, and set aside to marinate for about 30 minutes.

In a large salad bowl, combine the marinated chickpeas, lettuce, cucumbers, carrots, and salame. Drizzle the remaining vinaigrette (about ½ cup) over the top and toss to coat evenly. Using a vegetable peeler, shave the cheese over the top. Serve at once.

# Insalata di spinaci con pancetta croccante

## SPINACH SALAD WITH WARM PANCETTA VINAIGRETTE

This is a variation on the classic French *salade frisée aux lardons et oeufs*, but much less tricky because there are no poached eggs. Try to find very young spinach—the leaves will be tender and will look better on the plate—and be sure to rinse it well to remove any grit. The only crunch you want here is the pancetta in the warm vinaigrette.   SERVES 4

**WARM PANCETTA VINAIGRETTE**

¼ POUND PANCETTA, SLICED ¼ INCH THICK AND CUT INTO STRIPS ABOUT ¼ INCH WIDE

¾ CUP OLIVE OIL

2 TABLESPOONS RED WINE VINEGAR

1 TABLESPOON BALSAMIC VINEGAR

FRESHLY GROUND BLACK PEPPER

ABOUT ½ POUND FRESH WHITE OR CREMINI MUSHROOMS

8 CUPS SPINACH LEAVES, PREFERABLY SMALL

1 CUP THINLY SLICED GREEN ONIONS, INCLUDING GREEN PARTS

¼ TEASPOON SALT

2 HARD-BOILED EGGS, PEELED AND FINELY CHOPPED

FRESHLY GROUND BLACK PEPPER

To make the vinaigrette, in a small sauté pan, cook the pancetta in 1 tablespoon of the olive oil over medium heat, stirring occasionally, until somewhat crunchy, about 5 minutes. Add the remaining olive oil, both vinegars, and pepper to taste and mix well. Remove from the heat, and then rewarm over low heat just before needed.

Using a paring knife, trim away the stem ends on the mushrooms, and then wipe the mushrooms clean with damp paper towels. Slice the mushrooms ⅛ inch thick. You should have about 2 cups.

In a large salad bowl, toss the mushrooms with half of the warm vinaigrette. Add the spinach, green onions, and salt and drizzle the remaining vinaigrette over the top. Toss to coat all the ingredients evenly.

Divide the salad among individual plates. Distribute the eggs evenly over the salads, and then grind a little pepper over each salad. Serve at once.

# Insalata di ficchi, prosciutto, gorgonzola e nocciole

## SALAD OF FIGS, PROSCIUTTO, GORGONZOLA, AND HAZELNUTS

Nearly everyone enjoys the classic combination of figs and prosciutto. Here, that iconic pair moves into the salad realm, with the addition of greens, toasted nuts, and crumbled Gorgonzola cheese. You can vary the recipe by trading out sweeter hazelnuts for more bitter walnuts in the salad and walnut oil for the hazelnut oil in the vinaigrette. Black Mission figs are good here, though other types, such as Brown Turkey or Adriatic, would work as well. You can also halve the figs, brush the cut sides with olive oil, and grill them, cut sides down, over a charcoal fire or on a stove-top grill pan just until lightly marked. **SERVES** 4 to 6

**BALSAMIC AND HAZELNUT OIL VINAIGRETTE**
2 TABLESPOONS TOASTED HAZELNUT OIL
¼ CUP OLIVE OIL
2 TABLESPOONS ARTISANAL BALSAMIC VINEGAR
SALT

¼ CUP HAZELNUTS
4 HANDFULS OF SALAD GREENS, INCLUDING ARUGULA,
    RADICCHIO, AND A FEW FRESH MINT LEAVES, TORN
    INTO BITE-SIZED PIECES
SALT AND FRESHLY GROUND BLACK PEPPER
6 RIPE FIGS, CUT INTO QUARTERS THROUGH
    THE STEM END
3 OUNCES THINLY SLICED PROSCIUTTO, CUT INTO
    STRIPS ABOUT 1 ½ INCHES LONG AND ¼ INCH WIDE
¼ POUND GORGONZOLA CHEESE, CRUMBLED

To make the vinaigrette, in a small bowl, whisk together both oils and the vinegar. Whisk in salt to taste.

Preheat the oven to 325°F. Spread the hazelnuts in a single layer in a pie pan and toast in the oven until fragrant and the color begins to deepen, about 10 minutes. Transfer the warm nuts to a kitchen towel and rub between your palms to remove the skins. Don't worry if bits of skin remain. Coarsely chop the nuts, place in a small bowl, add 2 tablespoons of the vinaigrette, and set aside to macerate for about 15 minutes.

In a bowl, combine the salad greens and macerated nuts with some of the vinaigrette, season with salt and pepper, and toss to coat the greens lightly. Divide among individual plates. Top each salad with the figs, prosciutto, and Gorgonzola, dividing them evenly. Drizzle the remaining vinaigrette evenly over the top and serve at once.

# Insalata di arance, cipolle e coppa

**SALAD OF ORANGES, ONIONS, AND COPPA**

This salad, with minor variations, appears all over the Mediterranean. Sometimes chopped mint or parsley is strewn over the top at the last minute. The *coppa* provides a harmonious meaty, chewy contrast to the tart citrus, and its mild heat is accentuated by the red pepper in the dressing. **SERVES** 4

**HOT PEPPER–CITRUS DRESSING**

6 TABLESPOONS EXTRA VIRGIN OLIVE OIL,
   OR AS NEEDED

1 TEASPOON RED PEPPER FLAKES

2 TABLESPOONS FRESH LEMON JUICE, OR AS NEEDED

1/2 TEASPOON FINELY MINCED GARLIC (OPTIONAL)

SALT

FRESHLY GROUND BLACK PEPPER (OPTIONAL)

1 SMALL RED ONION, SLICED PAPER-THIN

3 LARGE NAVEL ORANGES OR 2 SMALL GRAPEFRUITS

4 HANDFULS OF MESCLUN OR BABY LETTUCES

1/4 POUND THINLY SLICED *COPPA*, CUT INTO STRIPS
   ABOUT 1/4 INCH WIDE

To make the dressing, in a small saucepan, warm the 6 tablespoons olive oil over medium heat until quite hot but not boiling. Drop in a pepper flake. If the flake skips on top of the oil and doesn't burn or sink, add the rest of the pepper flakes and remove from the heat. (If the flake sinks, wait for the oil to get hotter and repeat.) Let the pepper flakes steep in the oil for about 30 minutes, then strain through a fine-mesh sieve into a small bowl and let cool completely. (In Italy, this is called *olio santo*, or "holy oil.")

Whisk the 2 tablespoons lemon juice into the cooled oil, then whisk in the garlic and salt to taste. You might even want a bit of black pepper. If the dressing is too hot for you, add a little more olive oil and maybe a touch more lemon. (Pepper flakes vary wildly in heat level, and so do diners' tolerance for heat. You should have about 1/2 cup dressing. You will need only half of it for this salad. Reserve the remainder for another salad.)

In a small bowl, combine the onion and 1 tablespoon of the dressing, turning the onion slices to coat evenly. Set aside to macerate for 10 to 15 minutes while you prepare the citrus.

Working with 1 orange at a time, cut a thin slice off the top and bottom to reveal the flesh. Stand the orange upright and remove the peel in wide strips, cutting downward and following the contour of the fruit. Make sure to remove all of the white pith. Using a serrated knife, cut the oranges crosswise into 1/4-inch-thick slices. With a toothpick, push out any seeds from the slices. If using grapefruits, cut away the peel the same way. Then, holding each grapefruit over a bowl, cut along both sides of each segment, releasing the segments from the membrane and allowing them to drop into the bowl. Using the knife tip, pry out any seeds from the segments.

In a bowl, combine the greens with 2 to 3 tablespoons of the dressing and toss to coat evenly. Divide the greens evenly among individual plates. Arrange the citrus and onion over the greens. Top with the *coppa* and serve at once.

# Insalata de fagiolini, pomodori piccoli e prosciutto

## GREEN BEAN AND YELLOW BEAN SALAD WITH CHERRY TOMATOES AND PROSCIUTTO

An eye-catching mix of bright colors, this salad celebrates summertime flavors and the unique salty, rich character of a fine prosciutto. If you like, you can extend the portions by serving the salad on a bed of leafy greens. **SERVES** 4

GARLIC VINAIGRETTE (SEE SALAD WITH CUCUMBERS, CARROTS, CHICKPEAS, AND SALAME, PAGE 126)

SALT

2/3 POUND HARICOTS VERTS OR OTHER SLENDER, YOUNG GREEN BEANS, TRIMMED

2/3 POUND SLENDER, YOUNG WAX BEANS, TRIMMED

4 THIN SLICES PROSCIUTTO, CUT INTO NARROW STRIPS

16 CHERRY TOMATOES, CUT IN HALF

8 TO 10 FRESH BASIL LEAVES

Make the vinaigrette as directed and set aside.

Bring a saucepan filled with water to a boil and salt lightly. Add the green beans and boil until tender but still firm, 2 to 3 minutes. Drain, rinse under cold running water to halt the cooking and set the color, and drain again. Dry in a dish towel. Repeat with the wax beans.

In a salad bowl, combine the green and wax beans, prosciutto, and tomatoes. Stack the basil leaves, roll up the stack lengthwise, and cut crosswise to create fine shreds. Scatter the shreds over the salad. Drizzle with enough of the vinaigrette to coat lightly and toss to coat evenly. Serve at once.

# Piselli con prosciutto

**PEAS WITH PROSCIUTTO**

You know it is springtime in Rome when this dish is on the table. Fresh peas will vary in cooking time, with tender, young peas cooking quickly and older, starchier specimens needing more time, more liquid, and maybe a pinch of sugar. The rest of the year, you can make this dish with thawed frozen peas.

4 TABLESPOONS UNSALTED BUTTER

1 SMALL YELLOW ONION, MINCED

3 POUNDS PEAS, SHELLED (ABOUT 3 CUPS)

½ CUP CHICKEN BROTH

4 THIN SLICES PROSCIUTTO, CUT CROSSWISE INTO
  NARROW STRIPS

SALT AND FRESHLY GROUND BLACK PEPPER

In a sauté pan, melt the butter over low heat. Add the onion and cook, stirring occasionally, until softened and translucent, 8 to 10 minutes. Add the peas and broth, raise the heat to medium, and cook until the peas are tender, 1 to 3 minutes, depending on their age. Add the prosciutto strips and cook, stirring occasionally, until they curl, just a few minutes. Remove from the heat and season to taste with salt and pepper.

Transfer to a warmed serving dish and serve at once.

# SHOP
# AND
# SERVE
ANTIPASTI

SIMPLE SALUMI PAIRINGS

# PERFECT MATCHES

SOMETIMES THE SIMPLEST pairing makes the biggest impression. These complementary combinations keep the salumi at center stage.

- Serve prosciutto, salame, or *coppa* slices alongside melon, fig, peach, mango, Fuyu persimmon, or pear slices.

- Alternate *coppa* slices and grapefruit segments on a bed of arugula and drizzle with extra virgin olive oil.

- Alternate *coppa* and pear slices on a plate and top with crumbled Gorgonzola cheese and chopped toasted walnuts.

- Arrange *sopressata* slices and shaved Parmesan cheese on a bed of arugula and drizzle with extra virgin olive oil.

# Radicchio all'aceto balsamico e pancetta croccante

### RADICCHIO WITH BALSAMIC VINAIGRETTE AND PANCETTA

Pancetta and balsamic vinegar provide the balance in this recipe: the pancetta is sweet and salty, while the vinegar is mellow from years of aging, yet still acidic enough to stand up to radicchio's bitter edge. The radicchio is blanched, then broiled or baked in a hot oven (see variation). Alternatively, you can wrap the radicchio in prosciutto or pancetta, grill or bake it, and then drizzle it with balsamic vinegar just before serving.   SERVES 4

SALT

4 SMALL HEADS RADICCHIO

¼ CUP EXTRA VIRGIN OLIVE OIL

2 TABLESPOONS AGED BALSAMIC VINEGAR

FRESHLY GROUND BLACK PEPPER

WARM PANCETTA VINAIGRETTE (SEE SPINACH SALAD
    WITH WARM PANCETTA VINAIGRETTE, PAGE 127)

Preheat the broiler.

Bring a large pot filled with water to a boil. Lightly salt the water and then drop in the radicchio. Cook the radicchio for 2 minutes, pushing the heads under the water as needed to keep them immersed most of the time. Drain well and press gently to squeeze out excess moisture. If the heads are large, cut them in half through the stem end.

In a small cup, whisk together the olive oil and balsamic vinegar.

Place the radicchio on a broiler pan and sprinkle with salt and pepper. Brush with some of the olive oil mixture. Broil for 3 minutes, then turn and brush with more of the oil mixture and broil until the radicchio is golden and tender, about 3 minutes longer.

Transfer the radicchio to a warmed platter or individual plates and spoon the warm vinaigrette over the top. Serve at once.

*Baked Variation:* Omit the pancetta vinaigrette. Preheat the oven to 400°F. Oil a baking dish large enough to accommodate the radicchio in a single layer without crowding. Blanch the radicchio and drain as directed, then cut the heads in half through the stem end. Wrap each half with a slice of pancetta or prosciutto and arrange in the prepared dish. Spoon the oil and vinegar mixture over the top. Bake until golden and tender, about 15 minutes. Serve at once.

# Gatto di patate alla napoletana

## MASHED POTATO CAKE FROM NAPLES

In eighteenth-century Naples, noble families often employed French chefs to cook for their families and for whenever they entertained. *Gatto di patate*, a mashed potato gratin filled with salami, peas, and mozzarella cheese, is a product of this long-ago French presence in the Neapolitan kitchen. Although *gatto* is most commonly recognized as the Italian word for "cat," here it is instead a corruption of the French *gâteau*, or "cake." Serve this full-flavored dish alongside a simple veal scaloppine, roast chicken, or grilled fish. SERVES 6

### MASHED POTATOES

3 POUNDS RUSSET OR YUKON GOLD POTATOES

SALT

3/4 CUP GRATED PECORINO CHEESE

2 EGGS, LIGHTLY BEATEN

6 TABLESPOONS UNSALTED BUTTER

1/2 CUP WHOLE MILK, OR AS NEEDED

FRESHLY GROUND BLACK PEPPER

### FILLING

1/4 POUND *SOPRESSATA*, PEELED AND FINELY DICED

1 CUP SHELLED PEAS, COOKED IN BOILING WATER JUST UNTIL TENDER AND DRAINED

1/2 POUND FRESH MOZZARELLA CHEESE, DICED

ABOUT 1 CUP TOMATO SAUCE, CANNED OR HOMEMADE (SEE NOTE, PAGE 140)

1 CUP TOASTED BREAD CRUMBS (SEE MACARONI WITH THREE CHEESES, MORTADELLA, AND VEGETABLES, PAGE 89)

EXTRA VIRGIN OLIVE OIL FOR DRIZZLING

To make the mashed potatoes, if you are using russet potatoes, preheat the oven to 400°F. Prick the potato skins in a few places with a fork, place on a rimmed baking sheet, and bake until very soft, about 1 hour. Let the potatoes cool just until they can be handled. Then cut them in half, scoop out the flesh into a ricer or food mill, discarding the skins, and pass the flesh through the ricer or mill into a bowl. Or, scoop them directly into the bowl and mash with a potato masher as smoothly as possible.

If using Yukon Gold potatoes, peel them, cut into chunks, and place in a saucepan with water to cover generously. Salt lightly, bring to a boil over high heat, reduce the heat to medium, and cook until tender, about 20 minutes. Drain well, then pass them through a ricer or a food mill placed over a bowl, or mash with a potato masher as smoothly as possible.

Add the pecorino cheese, eggs, butter, and milk to the potatoes and knead together with a spoon or your hands to make a soft puree. Season with 1 1/2 teaspoons salt and a few grinds of pepper. Set aside. CONTINUED ▶

Preheat the oven to 350°F. Oil a 9-by-12-by-2-inch baking or a 10-inch round baking dish or pie dish.

To make the filling, in a bowl, combine the *sopressata*, peas, and mozzarella and mix well. Add just enough of the tomato sauce to bind the mixture together.

Sprinkle the bottom of the prepared baking dish evenly with ½ cup of the bread crumbs. Spoon half of the mashed potatoes into the dish, patting them down to form an even layer. Spread the filling evenly over the potato layer. Top with the remaining potatoes, again patting them to form an even layer. Drizzle with olive oil and top with the remaining ½ cup bread crumbs.

Bake the potato cake until golden, about 40 minutes. Remove from the oven and let rest for at least 8 to 10 minutes before serving. Cut into servings and serve warm or at room temperature.

*Note:* To make tomato sauce, place 1 can (28 ounces) plum tomatoes and their juices in a food processor and process until finely chopped but not liquefied. Transfer to a heavy saucepan and stir in ½ cup tomato puree. Place over low heat, bring to a simmer, and cook, stirring often, until the sauce is slightly thickened, about 20 minutes. Season to taste with salt and pepper and stir in 2 tablespoons unsalted butter, cut into small pieces (or substitute 2 tablespoons extra virgin olive oil). If the tomatoes are tart, add a pinch of sugar. If you want the sauce to have an herbal undertone, stir in 6 fresh chopped basil leaves. For a richer, sweeter, thinner sauce, stir in ½ to ¾ cup heavy cream. Remove from the heat. You should have about 3 cups sauce. It will keep, tightly covered, in the refrigerator for up to 4 days.

# Index

# Table of Equivalents

The exact equivalents in the following tables have been rounded for convenience.

## LIQUID/DRY MEASURES

| U.S. | METRIC |
| --- | --- |
| ¼ teaspoon | 1.25 milliliters |
| ½ teaspoon | 2.5 milliliters |
| 1 teaspoon | 5 milliliters |
| 1 tablespoon (3 teaspoons) | 15 milliliters |
| 1 fluid ounce (2 tablespoons) | 30 milliliters |
| ¼ cup | 60 milliliters |
| ⅓ cup | 80 milliliters |
| ½ cup | 120 milliliters |
| 1 cup | 240 milliliters |
| 1 pint (2 cups) | 480 milliliters |
| 1 quart (4 cups, 32 ounces) | 960 milliliters |
| 1 gallon (4 quarts) | 3.84 liters |
| 1 ounce (by weight) | 28 grams |
| 1 pound | 454 grams |
| 2.2 pounds | 1 kilogram |

## LENGTH

| U.S. | METRIC |
| --- | --- |
| ⅛ inch | 3 millimeters |
| ¼ inch | 6 millimeters |
| ½ inch | 12 millimeters |
| 1 inch | 2.5 centimeters |

## OVEN TEMPERATURE

| FAHRENHEIT | CELSIUS | GAS |
| --- | --- | --- |
| 250 | 120 | ½ |
| 275 | 140 | 1 |
| 300 | 150 | 2 |
| 325 | 160 | 3 |
| 350 | 180 | 4 |
| 375 | 190 | 5 |
| 400 | 200 | 6 |
| 425 | 220 | 7 |
| 450 | 230 | 8 |
| 475 | 240 | 9 |
| 500 | 260 | 10 |